unshackled

DR. ELIZABETH STEVENS

with THOMAS JEFFRIES

unshackled

Finding God's Freedom from Trauma

FOCUS
ON THE FAMILY.

A Focus on the Family Resource
Published by Tyndale House Publishers

Unshackled: Finding God's Freedom from Trauma
© 2022 Elizabeth Stevens. All rights reserved.

A Focus on the Family book published by Tyndale House Publishers, Carol Stream, Illinois 60188

Focus on the Family and the accompanying logo and design are federally registered trademarks of Focus on the Family, 8605 Explorer Drive, Colorado Springs, CO 80920.

Tyndale and Tyndale's quill logo are registered trademarks of Tyndale House Ministries.

Cover photograph of swans copyright © imageBROKER/Erhard Nerger/Getty Images. All rights reserved.

Designed by Sarah Susan Richardson

For information about special discounts for bulk purchases, please contact Tyndale House Publishers at csresponse@tyndale.com, or call 1-855-277-9400.

ISBN 978-1-64607-037-4

Printed in the United States of America

28 27 26 25 24 23 22
7   6   5   4   3   2   1

contents

Introduction *1*

introduction

The first thing I recall after regaining consciousness was total blindness, followed immediately by searing pain. My head was aching and my jaw was throbbing, clenched so tightly that I thought my teeth had been knocked out.

It was the summer of 2015, and I'd been descending from atop Longs Peak in Colorado's Rocky Mountain National Park. The weather was beautiful that day, and a friend and I had reached the summit by sunrise. We were on our way back down the mountain, crossing a sloping field of boulders, when I stumbled and fell.

My friend was ahead of me and didn't witness my fall, but I can remember that both my hands were caught tightly in the straps of my hiking poles, and I was unable to catch myself before I fell headfirst into a large rock below me.

Everything went white. My mind flashed back to my one previous life-threatening experience: As a child, I had slipped underwater in a swimming pool. I knew I couldn't breathe and that I was about to drown, until someone noticed me struggling and pulled me back to the surface.

On that mountainside field of boulders, I felt like that drowning child again. *I can't breathe.* My life seemed to be fading away.

As I gradually came to, I touched my face and realized that my eyes were covered with blood. I started to wipe it off, discovering that I wasn't blind after all. Blood was flowing out of a head wound above my left eye. I was in shock, dizzy, and nauseated, but I managed to convert my buff—a head covering favored by mountain climbers—into a bandage.

A park ranger quickly arrived on the scene and told me I needed to get down the mountain as soon as possible. He said that the nearest rescue team was busy assisting with a car accident, so my friend and I would need to descend on our own.

My neck was unsteady, and I had likely experienced whiplash, but I was able to make it back to the car without falling again. As we'd encountered groups of hikers on their way up the mountain, I'd been surprised at the looks of stark horror I'd seen in their eyes. When I saw my reflection in the car, I suddenly understood the reason for them. I looked like a warrior out of the movie *Braveheart*, my face crimson with blood and a makeshift bandage wrapped around my head. My friend drove me to the emergency room in a nearby town, where they cleaned my wound and stitched me up. They also took a CT scan that apparently showed no immediate concerns. Then they sent me home.

I didn't realize it at the time, but I had suffered a traumatic brain injury (TBI). It wasn't the first time I'd experienced serious trauma. Unfortunately, it also wouldn't be the last.

At the time, I had no understanding of the journey that lay ahead of me, the time I'd spend struggling to regain some sense of normalcy. My body no longer had the same capabilities as before, and my mind wasn't much better. The person I had been before the injury seemed to have vanished.

Reflecting on this experience years later, even as I still mourned for the person who'd been lost, I began to realize what I've gained along the way. I started to recognize how God has used this journey to soften my heart and help me more fully experience emotions I once pushed aside. He's used the trauma that tore my soul to bring healing in areas of my life that I'd never even realized were broken.

• • •

When most people hear the word *trauma*, they often picture serious, life-threatening situations—a military ambush, a school shooting, someone being trapped in a burning building. Others might think of victims of violent crime, abuse, or sexual assault. We might even remember those whose job it is to step in and help—the medical workers, the soldiers, the first responders, the people whose next shift on duty could bring them face to face with a deadly car crash, a natural disaster, or cardiac arrest.

But much trauma is unnoticed. Trauma can occur whenever someone is overwhelmed, like when they narrowly avoid a head-on collision, face a serious illness, or experience ongoing harassment or bullying. Repressed childhood trauma can rear its head years later when an individual faces certain triggering events. Constant threats of danger or harm are enough to trigger traumatic responses. (The fear of domestic violence, for example, can sneak up on a person in their own home.)

The *Diagnostic and Statistical Manual of Mental Disorders* (DSM-5), the American Psychiatric Association's pre-eminent manual on mental disorders, says that individuals can develop post-traumatic stress disorder (PTSD) merely from being exposed to someone *else's* trauma, like witnessing a traumatic event or learning that a close friend or loved one has faced one.[1]

As we consider the wider landscape of trauma, we begin to recognize that it may lurk all around us. It's a frightening thought, to be sure, but having this larger view of the nature of trauma allows us to better recognize and navigate its effects in our own lives.

The experience of trauma can cause feelings of loss, hopelessness, and helplessness. It can also affect how we see God and ourselves. When we clearly identify the trauma in our lives and how it affects us, we can better address the resulting dysfunctional thought patterns and behaviors that lead to harmful barriers in our relationships, faith, careers, and more.

• • •

I never intended to spend my professional career working with trauma patients. This wasn't even on my radar during my time in medical school. I studied medicine because I wanted to help hurting people get better, to get to the root causes of their health problems.

I joined the United States Air Force because I come from a military family. I know the people. I know the culture. And I wanted to help men and women who serve our country. As I progressed through my clinical rotations, I discovered just how little time most physicians are able to spend with their patients. I realized that my goal of getting to know patients on a deep level—and helping to find the root causes of their health problems—was not meant to be.

But my initial disappointment turned to relief during my final rotation in medical school. Psychiatry, I discovered, was where I needed to be. In this work, I could spend significant time with my patients. I could listen to their stories, and as they faced their pain, I could help free them from their inner turmoil. I sensed that God had created me for this purpose. I felt truly inspired for the first time during my years in medical school.

I continued my psychiatry training in the Air Force, and my sense of calling toward this profession only increased. In the Air Force, I encountered patients dealing with trauma and PTSD. I evaluated service members flown in from combat zones and wounded soldiers in burn centers—men and women, often just returning from deployment, who'd experienced some truly horrible situations.

I worked at military facilities, with the Department of Veterans Affairs (VA), at university hospitals, in detention centers, and in children's clinics. I treated patients dealing with bipolar disorders, psychosis, depression, anxiety, delirium, substance abuse, eating disorders, and more. I learned how to rule out medical problems that masquerade as psychiatric symptoms. And, thanks to a fellowship I received through the Air Force, I spent a year away from military duties training to be a child and adolescent psychiatrist. That fellowship was a great opportunity to help not just individuals but entire families.

The fellowship brought me to Colorado, and the mountains of Colorado are what brought me to my knees. When I fell headfirst into a boulder on that sunny morning on Longs Peak, my career focus shifted again. I sustained a traumatic brain injury, but I started to realize that the training I'd received and the tools I'd gained were not enough to restore my own health.

It was puzzling: I had learned a lot about trauma via my education and my practice, but now I was experiencing it for myself. And I didn't have any answers.

• • •

This book is about how I found healing after traumatic events—and how I've helped others find healing from theirs. I have journeyed alongside patients plagued with severe anxiety and psychosis, watching as they've progressed from a state of barely being able to leave their homes to a state of being employed and even helping others on their journeys. I've witnessed how resilient people can be.

This book is for anyone who's experienced trauma, whether physical or emotional. Military members, civilians, first responders. Parents and children. People who simply want to be better community leaders, coworkers, and friends. Perhaps you're reading this book because you've had a personal encounter with trauma, either recently or in the distant past. Or maybe you have a close friend or loved one who's struggling with the ongoing effects of a traumatic experience. Whatever your exposure to trauma, I trust that this book has something for you.

Experience has taught me that everyone has his or her own path to wholeness. In my work, I emphasize strategies for dealing with life's stressors and the importance of self-care, but there is no set protocol that works for everyone. Recovering from trauma requires patience, flexibility, and consistency.

Through my journey, I've learned that God can transform a heart traumatized by fear into one full of compassion. My goal in this book is to guide readers out of isolation and onto a path of healing, wholeness, and resilience.

This book is also for those who don't yet realize they are suffering. You might have received a copy from someone who cares about you. If that describes you, you'll need to start with the recognition that denial is a powerful defense mechanism and one of the most effective tactics of our enemy, the devil. When we deny the truth about our past trauma, we keep it buried deep, where it will continue to fester. The longer we ignore it, the more it will continue to impact our lives. How can we heal from a situation if we refuse to acknowledge its existence?

Are you experiencing restlessness, anger, resentment, or defensiveness? Is it sometimes difficult to be alone with your own thoughts? You may fall into the category of denial, never having viewed your experiences as particularly traumatic. You may dismiss even the possibility that they've affected you in a significant way. That's actually quite understandable: The last thing most folks want to do after enduring a terrible experience or loss of control is to revisit it. But honest recognition is a necessary first step toward healing.

• • •

This book will help you deal with the traumatic experiences that have stolen your sense of freedom, fostered bitterness and anger, or created fertile soil for addiction. We'll examine the stories of several of my patients to see how they've been able to overcome their traumas through spiritual and group support, various therapies and medications, and a recognition of lifelong barriers. The names of these patients, along with some specific details, have been changed to protect their privacy. By sharing these stories with you, I hope to provide comfort and encouragement through the process of looking at those who have overcome similar levels of hardship and adversity.

You'll read about Rachel, a military veteran who came to me looking for help with her PTSD. She was having trouble in her relationships and struggling with underlying anger on a daily basis. She had traumatic flashbacks, irritability, and serious anxiety. As we discussed her personal history, I learned that she had suffered years of sexual abuse growing up—a situation that had prompted her to join the military in order to escape. What's more, her family members had abused drugs for as long as she could remember, to the point that it had almost been considered a badge of honor in their home.

You'll meet Chris, a seasoned firefighter whom I met through a support group for first responders and veterans. He has seen some of the worst tragedies possible trying to rescue people trapped in burning buildings, including babies who didn't end up making it out alive. He's tried to resuscitate many fire victims, and he hasn't always been successful. He often used to blame himself for those who did not survive, and he came to the point where the burden was a pressure he could no longer bear.

You'll learn about Jill, a woman who had spent her entire life trapped in a cycle of guilt and shame. Her childhood had left her convinced that she was worthless. Her father had sexually abused her and her sister growing up, and their mother had never acknowledged the abuse or done anything to stop it. Jill coped by trying to block the memories, at least until she began to experience PTSD symptoms after the birth of her first child. She was hypervigilant and overcome with fear. She couldn't trust any man to treat her with respect, to treat her as anything other than a sexual object. She thought her husband was always looking at other women. She was plagued by fears of her husband betraying her, even though there was no evidence to support these thoughts.

I'll also share my own journey. After my TBI, I visited every specialist in the book. I tried every therapy or medication I thought might help. Each new treatment was supposed to be the one that would finally give me hope, but none of them worked. The more positive I felt about a treatment, the more I crashed into despair when it failed. It got to the point where my doctors started asking what *I* thought I needed. So many experts, so little information! And so little help.

I tried to rely on God. I listened to the whole Bible and poured out my heart in prayer. I told God that it didn't matter if I recovered, as long as I had a close relationship with Him. I wanted to believe that, but each day was a new struggle. I easily slipped into impatience and frustration. I couldn't take my mind off my misery, or my inability to work, or my headaches.

I could not ignore my deep longing to be *well*.

Each day I would wake up hoping that this was finally the day when I could read a book or catch up on my email again. But every day became the same nightmare of boredom, hopelessness, and helplessness.

What was I supposed to do?

Was there anything I could do?

denial

The days, weeks, and months that followed my traumatic brain injury were a haze of sleep, recurring nausea, involuntary inactivity—and then more trauma. Everything changed as a result of my injury, especially my identity and my sense of self-worth. In an instant, I was transformed from a high-achieving United States Air Force major and psychiatrist into someone who could no longer read or control my own emotions—or, in essence, my own life.

My mother flew to Colorado right away to help care for me. We soon made another trip to the emergency room because I couldn't stop throwing up and certainly couldn't keep any food down. The doctors there sent me to my military base, where I could consult with my primary care physician. My doctor prescribed "brain rest," which meant no reading, no electronics, and no strenuous activity of any kind, mental or physical. I was told that I had no choice in the matter.

The instructions were easy to follow, at least at first. I spent most of the next month sleeping. Even having a simple conversation was very disconcerting—I couldn't find the words I wanted, and my memory was shot. I slurred my speech and couldn't retain information I'd just heard.

The military physician prescribed TBI rehabilitation, during which I would receive speech therapy as well as physical and occupational therapy. However, my queasiness, low energy, and inability to retain information made progress almost impossible. I could barely tolerate the car ride to my appointments. By the time I made it to the treatment center, I'd already be wracked with nausea.

I was also pretty oblivious to what was going on around me. In those first few weeks, I displayed a carefree, laid-back mentality I had never exhibited before. "What happened to my daughter?" my mother asked. It turned out that her daughter was in denial. At the time, I was still assuming that I would be back to work and to normalcy in no time.

My mother and I got a revealing glimpse into my current state when a speech therapist read me a story to help assess any cognitive deficits I might have. It was a brief story, just a few sentences, about a boy who threw three rocks into a lake. As soon as she finished reading, she asked me how many rocks the boy threw. I racked my brain as hard as I could, but . . . nothing. I could not recall the number. My mom said that that was the moment she realized my recovery was going to be a long haul.

So much for all my postgraduate schooling. The last day I was in therapy, the TBI rehab program coordinator had a talk with my mother and me. She said I might have to consider the possibility that the Air Force would retire me. I didn't want to entertain that possibility, and I told my mom there was no way it would happen. I was completely unable to grasp the gravity of my situation. I remained convinced that I would bounce back.

In addition to my rehabilitation program, I still needed surgery to repair my broken nose. The plastic surgeon was unable to complete the repairs due to unexpectedly finding a large hole in my septum. (When it rains, it pours!)

When I awoke from the anesthesia, the surgeon told me that I'd need to schedule another surgery because he hadn't been prepared for the additional damage he had encountered. I was (obviously) not looking forward to another operation, especially since I had reacted to my first surgery with a sleepless night of intense nausea and vomiting because I'd had a reaction to the anesthesia. To top it off, the rehab center told me that I couldn't tolerate any more therapy at that time and that it would be best if I didn't come back until after the second surgery.

So, another setback. Another month of waiting. Nothing to do except rest.

I couldn't watch television or even look at my phone because it might trigger more extreme nausea. I went from climbing mountains to walking at an extremely slow pace, and even then only for short distances. Carrying on a conversation for longer than ten minutes left me exhausted, and when I got tired, my speech slurred. My appetite decreased, and I was losing both weight and strength. My good attitude was just about the only thing I had going for me, but that's probably because I was still in denial about my recovery. I simply couldn't process the seriousness of my situation. Besides, what could I really do? Not only was I being ordered to rest, but my body would give out on me if I didn't. I trusted that God would take care of me, and I remained hopeful that all this was temporary.

● ● ●

Denial hinders healing. When people refuse to accept the reality of a situation, it prevents them from taking the necessary steps to deal with their trauma. Denial is the first stop on legendary psychiatrist Elisabeth Kübler-Ross's well-known model of the five stages of grief. (The other four stages are anger, bargaining, depression, and acceptance.)

There are, however, certain circumstances in which denial can serve a helpful purpose. Sometimes it can give us a little time to process an extremely distressing event without going into a tailspin. In my case, it likely helped me in the initial healing process by insulating me from extreme anxiety and worry over the potential long-term repercussions of my TBI. It gave my body the chance to begin healing without excess stress hormones or difficulty relaxing. It was as if my mind and body were in a forced state of rest.

But while denial may be helpful for a short time, it can impede the recovery process if it lingers too long. It becomes toxic when it prevents people from making progress, leaving emotions unprocessed and keeping sufferers from seeking the help they need. I began to realize that this sort of toxic denial was what I was experiencing.

I've listened to law enforcement officers and other first responders share stories about all the horrific things they've witnessed and follow them up with the almost stubborn assertion that none of it ever really affected them. I've had military patients who have endured the horrors of combat tell me that the experience never bothered them.

Wait . . . what?

How can you witness horrific evil or suffering and remain unaffected? It's important to note that a good number of those patients have failed marriages and few close friendships, if any. Many also admit that they haven't experienced significant peace or joy for years.

It never really bothered me.

I would argue that these people have developed innate protective mechanisms that help them keep and maintain emotional distance from the terrible things they've seen. But these mechanisms have negatively affected their personal lives. Perhaps the most common one is denial. They may not necessarily be denying that trauma occurred but rather that they have been or continue to be influenced by it in any detrimental way.

To be clear, the detrimental influence of trauma isn't always manifested as PTSD. It could be manifested as a simple change in thought patterns or behavior. For example, a seasoned paramedic might not recognize the symptoms or significant effects of trauma upon learning that his wife and daughter have been involved in a car accident, but years later he might recognize the impact the event has had on him when called to the scene of a car wreck with another woman or child involved.

When our bodies' systems are overwhelmed, we are forced to make a choice—especially if a traumatic experience is personal and cuts to our core. We can choose to process the trauma with God and those we trust, or we can choose to ignore it and move on. It's like having a stallion stampeding through your soul: You can try to harness the trauma in search of deep healing, or you can let it run wild and wreak havoc.

Here's another way to put it: If you do nothing and continue on in denial, the enemy can use your trauma to unleash reckless, destructive power in your life. But if you call on God's mercy and power, He can redirect what the enemy intends for evil to bring about transformation, character refinement, and healing.

• • •

Trauma and its resulting effects can be so overwhelming and painful that we'll do everything possible to minimize the helplessness and powerlessness we feel. Sometimes this involves altering our memories, suppressing past events as if they never happened, or avoiding the places, thoughts, or feelings that remind us of our trauma. We create distractions and comforts to ease our pain and suffering. We try to evade the cruelty we see around us or even the cruelty we see in ourselves. We try to pretend the pain isn't there. These are the strategies of those who are in denial.

Heuristics, or mental shortcuts, are methods people use to make a quick decision when there's little time to consider all the available information. An educated guess is one example of a heuristic. When we try to make sense of trauma in the moment, our brains try to take these little shortcuts in an effort to fill in the gaps. The problem is that this process often leads to faulty reasoning in the future. Heuristics sometimes lead people to make decisions based on strong associated emotions, like when a child fears all dogs because she was once bitten by one. Her brain takes a shortcut to her fear through the neighborhood of that one experience.

One of my patients, Laura, was a case of heuristics gone wrong. Laura was molested by a religious leader when she was a child. For sixty years, she kept that trauma to herself, never dealing with it or considering how it might continue to affect her many years later. (In fact, I was the first person she ever told about the abuse.) One outcome was that she harbored a lifelong prejudice against all clergy members. She refused to believe in God. This unresolved trauma shaped the way she viewed believers in Christ for the rest of her life.

While heuristics can help us make snap decisions in the heat of the moment, they can also introduce errors in thinking, leading to inaccurate thought patterns throughout life. A shortcut doesn't always get us to the right place.

In Laura's case, she associated religious people with harm, applying her fear of one individual to every person of religious authority, including God. Clearly there were other factors and emotions involved, but Laura's manner of condensing her experience reflects a common pattern with trauma.

When denial is strong, faulty thought patterns are rarely addressed or even acknowledged—a situation that can persist for years or even decades.

I've treated several patients who experienced significant childhood traumas but didn't start exhibiting severe PTSD symptoms until their children left the home. The power of denial helped them manage long enough to raise their children, but it also preserved their wounds to the extent that the PTSD had become quite severe by the time they began processing their pasts. I've also counseled Vietnam veterans who maintained successful careers after the war only to develop severe PTSD once they retired.

Denial cannot be sustained indefinitely, and maintaining it takes a lot of energy. This is why many trauma sufferers seek constant distraction. It's why they are uncomfortable with quiet, with being alone with their thoughts.

When we're in denial, we remain vulnerable. The enemy knows how trauma affects us. He knows our vulnerabilities and the comforts we seek in order to distract ourselves from our distress and suffering. His goal is to keep us away from God and draw us to anything other than Him to find peace. The enemy wants us to remain isolated, our pain locked away. That way he can continue feeding us accusations, distorted thinking, and distrust.

But when we invite God to shine His light on our wounds, traumas, and hurts, the enemy has to leave. This is why confession and Christian community are so important. The enemy simply can't stay in that environment.

Denial keeps us from acknowledging our trauma to others, which prevents us from receiving their support and, eventually, our healing. The enemy wants us to remain trapped in denial, enslaved by its effects. The protective mechanisms we put in place, including denial, are not sustainable. They end up stealing our freedom and shrinking our worlds. This is the destructive nature of denial.

• • •

If you are in denial about your trauma, you might not recognize that you're in denial. Here are some signs that this might be what you're dealing with:

* You get angry, sad, irritable, or short tempered for no apparent reason.
* You stay isolated and allow few people, if any, into your immediate circle.
* You struggle with relationships—though you don't know why—and have difficulty connecting with others.
* You become defensive at the drop of a hat.
* Your loved ones beg you to seek help, but you don't think you have a problem.

Once you've recognized denial of trauma, it's time to start dealing with it:

* Try to develop better self-awareness. One exercise that I've found to be very effective is to ask a few people whom you trust and who know you well to list three positive qualities about you and three areas where you need improvement. Take notes, and look for a pattern among these observations. Have your friends noticed something about you that you haven't been able to admit to yourself before?

  In his classic book *The Screwtape Letters*, C. S. Lewis imagines two demons in conversation about how to best distract a new believer in Christ. Screwtape, the more experienced of the two, illustrates the power of self-deception: "You must bring [the new Christian] to a condition in which he can practise self-examination for an hour without discovering any of those facts about himself which are perfectly clear to anyone who has ever lived in the same house with him or worked in the same office."[1] Lewis recognized that those who are close to us can often easily pick up on characteristics or qualities that might take us months of therapy to uncover ourselves. This is why it's vital to be part of a safe and authentic community.

* Try to identify situations where people or things trigger, anger, or infuriate you. A *trigger* is something that sets off a fight-or-flight reaction, brings on PTSD symptoms, or produces excessive stress.

Sometimes such responses can arise from righteous anger regarding injustice, but they can also arise from sins within ourselves that we also see in others. People around us are often like mirrors, reflecting back both our goodness and our flaws. We can tend to react negatively toward people we see doing the same things that we struggle with.

* Reflect on any discomfort or restlessness you experience around certain people. If you identify any, talk with someone you trust about the situation or make an appointment with a counselor or therapist. Through these interactions, seek God's wisdom in helping you discern why you react the way you do.

We often miss the correlation between others' behavior and our own. If that is a pervasive pattern in your life, there's a good chance that something hidden is waiting to be uncovered. We must look to Jesus' wisdom in Matthew 7:3-5: "Why do you see the speck that is in your brother's eye, but do not notice the log that is in your own eye? Or how can you say to your brother, 'Let me take the speck out of your eye,' when there is the log in your own eye? You hypocrite, first take the log out of your own eye, and then you will see clearly to take the speck out of your brother's eye."

* Consider working with a professional counselor or therapist. It's important to remember that close relationships tend to stir up the most struggles. Those closest to

us are the ones who know us best; we tend to let down our guard more around loved ones than we do around coworkers or the general public. We also usually trust a spouse or close friend more than other people. Trauma, however, can make us less willing to trust those close to us. It can make us prone to defend ourselves from future hurt and resistant to exposing our vulnerabilities. This leads to a defensive mindset that makes it difficult to empathize with or even hear what other people are saying to us.

This is where a neutral observer like a professional counselor or therapist can help. And if you seek out marriage, family, or group counseling, the counselor can also guide difficult conversations and help each person effectively communicate what they might otherwise avoid processing. When emotions remain under control, the counselor can ensure that both parties listen appropriately and help tease out any underlying trauma that's been leading to conflict.

● ● ●

I spent the first few weeks after my mountain accident in denial about the severity of my TBI, and it was in the midst of that season of weakness that I suffered an even worse trauma. This second experience wounded not only my body but also my heart and soul. I went from temporary denial, which was actually helping me heal, to ongoing, toxic denial that left me in a loneliness I had never experienced before.

First, a little background. Many girls dream of a prince who will sweep her off her feet, provide for her, pursue her, and protect her with everything he has. That was definitely the case with me. I was waiting for a man who would respect me, honor me, and value my purity above his desires—a man who pursued God and never gave up. Even as I devoted years to my medical training and Air Force career, I still dreamed of finding a life partner and soul mate. But I never found anyone who met my criteria. I also never took the time to pursue anyone myself. After all, the man should pursue the woman . . . right?

Throughout my schooling and medical residency, I found life outside of work to be very lonely. Most of my friends were married and had kids, and it was hard to find people to hang out with outside of work. Once I moved to Colorado, I had more free time and finally decided to explore online dating. I normally gravitate toward people who enjoy the outdoors, so I connected with someone who loved the mountains as much as I did. He started pursuing me, and it felt good to be desired and have an adventure partner. In fact, it felt so good that I began ignoring the red flags in our relationship.

I was trying to fill the void of my loneliness, so my desire to be pursued, wanted, and appreciated overwhelmed my desire to wait for a spiritual leader, for someone who served God. I just didn't want to be alone anymore. When this man told me that waiting until marriage for sex was a deal breaker for him, I simply ignored it. I truly believed that I could change him into an amazing Christian—the kind of man I'd always wanted to marry.

Clearly, I had my motives in our relationship, but he had one too. He kept pressuring me, and one night he got what he wanted. It was my thirtieth birthday, and we had just completed one of the most difficult hikes in Colorado. We celebrated with a couple of glasses of wine. I was absolutely exhausted, and that night, his will won out. He took what was meant for my husband.

I felt like I had died inside, as if everything good in me was gone. I felt worthless, thinking that the only way I could redeem the situation was to make this man my husband. I teetered between not caring what happened and trying to do whatever it took to make him love me and marry me and pursue God. But the more I tried to make it work, the more I started drifting away from my own faith.

The relationship became toxic. It was a classic power struggle: the woman's desire to change a man versus the man's desire not to be controlled. I didn't realize how much this relationship was about finding my worth instead of finding a godly partner.

It wasn't until years later that I realized just how much of my identity I had once associated with my sexual purity. Indeed, for many years I had lived with a legalistic mentality: As long as the outside of the cup (my moral behavior) was impeccable, it didn't matter that on the inside I felt dirty and ashamed (see Matthew 23:25-26).

A spiritual barrier like this sort of self-righteousness can impact every aspect of life, preventing true healing from trauma. In my case, it led to a long series of poor choices that caused me to drift away from my true identity as a child of God. The cleansing power of Christ's sacrifice had already made me without blemish in God's eyes, but my quest to be lovable and worthy of a man led me to a dead end of darkness and pain.

In that dead end, however, I found something beautiful, something that I'd never realized I'd been missing. I found the true lover of my soul—a heavenly Father with open arms welcoming me into His embrace. I began to learn the difference between chasing after an imperfect mate and inviting Jesus to satisfy my deepest longings. While I'd been pressuring and cajoling my boyfriend to meet my needs, Jesus had always been there, offering Himself to me completely and without hesitation.

● ● ●

After my accident, I was in denial about certain aspects of my trauma, like recognizing how long the recovery from the TBI might take. But I was not in denial about my debilitating condition. I knew it was getting worse and that I needed to seek God's peace more than ever before, because the ultimate healing comes only from Him. I figured that the best first step to ensuring I could find peace and healing was to prioritize my relationship with Him. I still couldn't read, so I listened to my Bible app as much as possible. I wanted to draw closer to God and get my strength from His Word.

At the same time, I felt convicted about my relationship

with my boyfriend. I told him that I needed to follow God's plan, which meant that I could no longer engage in sex outside of marriage. I knew that this decision could spell the end of our relationship, but I simply had to put God first. While my boyfriend wasn't happy about my decision, he said that he would continue to stick with me, even after my traumatic brain injury on the mountain.

For several weeks, I resisted his pressure, but one night it became a physical struggle that I couldn't prevent. I don't remember the exact circumstances before it happened. (This is pretty common for someone experiencing post-traumatic stress.) What I do remember is that my boyfriend pulled me off my mattress and pushed me against the side of the bed. I tried to escape his grip, but I had little strength to fight back so soon after my injury. All I could do was cry and try to remain still until the attack was over. I never knew I could feel so humiliated, dehumanized, and powerless all at the same time.

I would never be the same, but the next day it somehow seemed as if nothing had happened. I can only conclude that my subconscious mind was in another kind of denial, doing everything possible to simply protect my sanity. I just couldn't handle the thought that someone I'd loved and trusted—someone I'd allowed in—could have violated me when I was at my weakest. Sadly, I blamed myself for what had happened. *It must have happened because I let him into my life,* I thought.

My demeanor quickly changed, and I began suffering

from insomnia, intense migraines, and mood swings. I was frequently angry and irritable. But I failed to connect the sexual assault to any of these symptoms because I wouldn't even let myself remember that it had happened.

This new denial was even greater than the first! It created a wound in my soul that only God could heal. It created feelings of distrust of everyone around me. I even doubted myself. *How did I not see this coming? How can I trust anyone not to hurt me? How can I trust that God will protect me?*

Taken together, my distrust, isolation, shame, and hidden trauma were fertile ground for a brutal case of PTSD—and this was all in addition to my traumatic brain injury and the resulting issues with memory and processing. I had no idea what I was in for. This new, deeper denial was creating a number of barriers that would entrench my trauma even further.

In the space of several weeks, I had now suffered two traumatic events. The first one had been bad enough, and I'd just started to recognize what it was doing to me. But I had no clue about the damage this second one would bring, nor could I imagine the long, dark journey that lay ahead of me.

REFLECTION

1. How have you dealt with traumatic events or significant stress in your life?
2. In what areas of your life do you feel the need to defend yourself?

3. When you spend time alone and become lost in your thoughts, what do you think about?
4. Is it difficult to be by yourself without distractions? Are there certain situations or conversations that you find yourself avoiding?

CHALLENGE

Identify three people in your life whom you trust, preferably those who know you best. Ask them to list three strengths about you as well as three areas in your life that need improvement. Do you see a pattern in these observations that you haven't ever admitted to yourself?

CHAPTER TWO

detachment

*"I will give you a new heart, and a new spirit I will
put within you. And I will remove the heart of stone
from your flesh and give you a heart of flesh."*

EZEKIEL 36:26

James is a combat veteran who served his country well only
to spend many years of his life trying to forget everything
he had seen and experienced. I was first introduced to him
through his wife. I had recently launched my Tribe curriculum meetings, which are Christ-centered group sessions I created for veterans and first responders. James's wife had heard
about a Tribe group that was meeting at a nearby church and
emailed me to say that her husband desperately needed just
such a group to help him porcess the combat trauma he had
endured in Vietnam. I told her to have him contact me so
I could share more specifics about the program. His email
arrived a short time later:

Please register me for this series. I served for a full year, which included about 1,500 total hours of very bloody and very violent combat missions as a helicopter pilot and aircraft commander. I rarely talk about it except with my combat buddies who also experienced it and/or flew with me (the few who survived with me, I mean). Talking about it is very emotional for me, so I don't—and probably won't— be able to do it in front of a group. But I will at least listen and contribute as much as I can handle.

True to his word, James introduced himself to the group at his first session and then sat quietly observing for the rest of the meeting. Over the following weeks, as more people in the group began to open up, he began to trust his fellow veterans with pieces of his story, including how the trauma resulting from his combat experience had affected him. He started feeling more at home in the group as he realized he was not alone regarding the challenges he'd faced. One night, after the group had wrapped up for the evening, he thanked me for creating the environment that had allowed him to process his trauma. "First, I was able to trust you, because I never felt pressured to share," he said. "And then I was able to start trusting others in the group."

Indeed, the biggest reason his walls eventually came down was because he saw that he wasn't alone. Everyone in the group was a veteran. They'd all taken the same oath. Many of them had seen combat. It had been many years since James had returned from war, but the group dynamic empowered him to engage in a form of healing therapy for the very first time, to tackle what he could now identify as PTSD.

The group session that brought perhaps the biggest shift for him occurred when he decided to process his memories of Vietnam in depth by acknowledging that God could heal his deep pains. He also learned to identify his *maladaptive behaviors*—the behaviors that prevented him from adapting to new or difficult circumstances. Maladaptive behaviors often begin after a life-altering or traumatic event, like combat.

When a Light Comes On

In my work with trauma sufferers, some of my favorite moments are when clients finally have a breakthrough, often after years spent in helplessness and confusion. These "lightbulb moments" happen when a client suddenly achieves a level of clarity that brings transformation and healing, like when they recognize the negative influence of a long-running behavior and decide to adopt a healthier course. It's in these moments that they often ask, "Why haven't I been told this before?"

I often point to a similar sort of breakthrough in the parable of the Prodigal Son, when the younger son looks longingly at the food given to the pigs. That's when he experiences his own lightbulb moment. As the Bible puts it, "he finally came to his senses" (Luke 15:17, NLT). When they happen for trauma sufferers, these moments are powerful and transformative.

James's lightbulb moment occurred when he finally let go of control, of trying to be his own protector, and decided to trust in God's love and forgiveness instead. That's when he received the peace that "surpasses all understanding" (Philippians 4:7). Prior to this session, when asked what brought him peace, his response suggested that he'd never experienced such a thing. "What is peace?" he said.

Initially, he hadn't been ready to confront his traumatic memories and emotional wounds, but the Tribe group sessions had helped give him the desire and the strength to trust God with the outcome. He knew that it was time to stop being in denial. It was time to dive in. It was time to get some help.

He acknowledged that he was haunted by visions of his fellow soldiers, many of them teenagers, lying in ruin. He couldn't escape from the soldier's mindset of waking up every morning with only one mission in mind—survival.

He also had emotional wounds that he'd never dealt with. For example, he'd lost a lot of buddies in Vietnam and had long felt that he somehow could—and should—have saved them. We explored one specific incident: the time his best friend had died in his arms. As he recalled the experience, he allowed himself to feel the emotions of anger, aggression, and apathy toward the enemy. He was finally able to process these emotions for the first time. The nature of war hadn't allowed him the time or environment to do that before, nor had he been equipped to deal with the tremendous suffering he witnessed almost daily.

The moment when his best friend died had been the moment James turned into a killing machine. From that point on, he decided that the enemy simply needed to die. When that internal switch flipped, it shut down his ability to recognize the value of human life. He detached himself emotionally. It was a necessary step, he concluded, if he wanted to survive and defend his fellow soldiers. They had to be the masters of their fate. No one else could be trusted. And the most effective way to control their environment was to eliminate the enemy.

He was forced to make life-and-death decisions in a split second, and the responsibility of those decisions weighed greatly on him. He suppressed his level of empathy to the degree that such situations could no longer overwhelm him, and this sense of detachment carried over into relationships in his post-military life, including his marriage.

But with the encouragement of his fellow veterans, he was able to repent of those decisions and receive God's forgiveness. He recognized that he was not a killing machine but rather a beloved child of God. He began to see how much God truly loves him. He began to release the pain, shame, and guilt of his past and replace them with God's forgiveness, love, and grace.

He couldn't see the havoc these memories and thoughts had wreaked in his life until he found true peace and joy for the first time. And as this helped him begin to process his past trauma, he discovered that he became able to bear his emotions and that they did not have to last forever.

Cognitive processing therapy (CPT) describes the concept of *manufactured emotions*. I helped James understand the relevance of this concept to his experiences. For someone who experiences a traumatic event, like combat, there are some natural, genuine emotions that occur as a result. Fear, sadness, anger—these are expected, natural emotions. On the other hand, traumatic events can also lead to certain artificial—or manufactured—emotions, like guilt, shame, and helplessness.

This doesn't mean that manufactured emotions don't feel real, but it does mean that we have some control over them. When genuine emotions remain unprocessed for one reason or another, they can intensify with each recurrence. As a coping mechanism resulting from such unprocessed emotions, trauma sufferers often end up manufacturing other emotions as they try to make sense of what happened to them. When emotions are manufactured, they can come out sideways at inopportune times.

As James learned to process his anger, his emotions lost their power over him. He did this by focusing his anger on the appropriate target—the fallen human race and the ugly nature of war—and addressing his memories instead of burying them. Rather than having to try to overcome his vulnerabilities through avoidance and denial and certain manufactured emotions, he was finally able to let go. He found peace. By accepting God as his protector, he no longer felt the burden of being strong for himself and everyone else. He learned to depend on God instead of himself.

His entire path in life began to shift during the group session when he recognized the distorted beliefs he'd held on to for years and decided it was time to confront his unspoken memories.

At the end of another one of our evenings together as a group, James wanted to talk to me. "What did you and God do to me?" he asked with a smile. He felt at peace, and he wanted to help others. He said that I was welcome to give other veterans his contact information. He'd gained newfound empathy for those who were suffering like he had been, and he now wanted to pay forward the comfort he'd received from God.

•   •   •

James had coped with his traumatic past by detaching from it as much as possible. He is far from alone in employing the coping mechanism of detachment. Anyone in a career field where they routinely encounter tragedy and loss knows its appeal. After all, how many people can witness unspeakable trauma day in and day out and not collapse from the weight of it?

But God desires to restore the hearts of His people. Our God is in the redemption business. We learn this from the prophet Ezekiel, who wrote about God's desire to remove Israel's heart of stone and replace it with a heart of flesh (Ezekiel 36:26). As traumas accrue, we tend to respond by trying to cover our wounds with protective walls or calluses—by building a heart of stone. And hardened hearts no longer react naturally to others' wounds.

We run the risk of becoming numb if we avoid reliving our own traumas or experiencing others' pain. In fact, *numb* is the word I've heard many first responders use to describe their emotional state when it comes to the horrific situations they've faced on the job. But it's not just emergency workers; everyone who's encountered multiple traumas is susceptible to this sort of detachment. This defense mechanism serves them for a while—until they realize just how hardened they've become.

When people avoid negative emotions, the fallout gradually affects their ability to experience positive emotions. For some, the desire to feel anything at all is so great that they gravitate toward high-risk or self-destructive activities, like skydiving or cutting. Others turn to alcohol and drugs to achieve a high that counteracts the dull, robotic emotional state they've adopted. A protective shell around a person's heart can also lead to reduced compassion for and connection with others.

How can we help soften the hearts of our friends who have built these protective shells? By having a willingness to reflect God's love and wisdom into their lives. The apostle Paul wrote about the influence we can have on others in 2 Corinthians 1:3-4: "Blessed be the God and Father of our Lord Jesus Christ, the Father of mercies and God of all comfort, who comforts us all in our affliction, so that we may be able to comfort those who are in any affliction, with the comfort with which we ourselves are comforted by God." Elsewhere, he again urges the church to demonstrate empathy for each other: "If there is any encouragement in Christ, any comfort from love, any participation in the Spirit, any affection and sympathy, complete my joy by being of the same mind, having the same love, being in full accord and of one mind" (Philippians 2:1-2).

There are few better comforters for people who are hurting than those of us who have suffered the same grief, who are already familiar with the pain. But being a comforter isn't easy. We naturally avoid reminders of our own trauma, especially if we don't yet know how to deal with it. And when given the opportunity to offer our compassion to someone else, we may be afraid that it will exhaust and deplete us by stirring up unwanted memories. Thus, we can be tempted to continue to detach ourselves from the suffering of others, missing out on the potential blessings and mutual healing that might result.

If you feel like you can help someone experiencing this sort of detachment from traumatic events, ask God to help you overcome your fears. Look to the example of Christ during His ministry. When He walked on the earth, He was greatly moved by the wounds of those around Him. He never shrank back from those who were hurting. He sat with the suffering and engaged with them in their distress. He knew that the love of the Father was far stronger than any suffering and could truly help people. Jesus had no fear that sharing in another's suffering would somehow worsen His own burden.

God can help you face your pain. If you refuse to acknowledge your wounds to yourself and before Him, it will be much harder to receive healing. And if you refuse to receive comfort because you just can't face the past, how will you be able to comfort others with God-given compassion? Moreover, if you can't face the painful past, how will you ever identify which harmful patterns of behavior have developed due to your trauma or which lies you've believed regarding the world around you, the people in your life, and your own identity?

• • •

Many first responders and military veterans don't know how to respond when their loved ones react to stressors that seem insignificant compared to what they themselves have faced, like crime, combat, sexual assaults, or horrific automobile accidents. Such hardened individuals aren't sure how "ordinary" people react to stress, and they may reveal their judgments about whether certain incidents warrant the strong negative reaction they're eliciting. Indeed, people who have experienced extreme malevolence and suffering have a difficult time relating to those who haven't, and they often struggle to empathize with loved ones' feelings.

My mother was a newborn intensive care nurse for more than thirty years. She encountered life-threatening situations on almost every shift. She saw countless newborns fight for survival—many of them in vain—and cared for many babies born to mothers addicted to cocaine, heroin, or methamphetamines. But when she needed to vent to let out her emotions, few people could understand or relate to her experiences. No one really wanted to hear about the tragedies she witnessed. She was rarely able to find the comfort she needed from friends or family members.

So she did what she felt like she had to do: She simply pushed down her emotions in order to move on and care for the next baby. I remember one night when she came home after a particularly rough twelve-hour shift. The dishes had piled up in the kitchen, and I made some excuse about being too tired to do them after an exhausting basketball practice. Not even looking at me, she said, "Did you just work for eight hours trying to keep a baby alive? Do the dishes!" And then she headed upstairs without another word.

James's survival mechanisms had been his response to the horrors of war. Nothing could have prepared him for his experiences in Vietnam, and he never wanted to revisit them. But no matter how hard he tried to forget what happened, he hadn't been able to escape the frequent flashbacks.

This particular coping mechanism—ignoring our memories and shielding our souls—is not limited to soldiers and emergency workers. Detachment can also occur after a romantic breakup, when we feel betrayed by a trusted friend, or when our perspective of the world is shaken. It's important to recognize the times in life when we try to hide or shove down our vulnerability and move on. Has this ever happened to you? If so, what habits or beliefs did you adopt? Did you vow to never love or trust so deeply again? Did you resolve to take control of your heart, pushing God and others out of the way?

We were created to be vessels of compassion, called to point lost and broken people to a love that heals all wounds. If we remain isolated, detached, and elusive, we'll miss out on the joy of achieving our own freedom, as well as the joy others will receive when we help them find theirs.

• • •

In the next few chapters, we'll explore several other common barriers to healing. As mentioned, denial and detachment are two examples of the sort of barriers we'll look at. These barriers can be psychological, spiritual, or physical in nature, or they might be barriers having to do with the communities we live in. All of them, however, hinder healing in some way.

Another barrier to healing is isolation. Isolation has become more pronounced in recent years, especially as many of us now engage with social media more than we do with the people around us. Whether by design or not, social media platforms cultivate a mentality among users that causes them to act like they have it all together. Online, we all put our best foot forward. Often, that's the only side of us that others see, even without major global events like the coronavirus pandemic, which suddenly kept us from meaningful face-to-face interaction. No matter the cause, the end result is isolation.

To make matters worse, we sometimes deny that barriers such as isolation or detachment even exist. If we do acknowledge their existence, we may be unwilling or unable to identify them as barriers in our own lives. *Sure, others might struggle with denial or isolation, but not me.*

We'll explore how even positive desires can become barriers if they are pursued to excess or are used to fill a void or satisfy a need that only God can. An example of this would be searching for a romantic partner to complete you—to find that ideal soul mate who will love you unconditionally. The desire for a spouse is certainly not a bad one, but it has disastrous implications when we expect the same kind of unconditional love and acceptance from one that only God can provide. When struggles and conflicts arise in a relationship—and they inevitably will—this realization will hit home. Hard.

We'll also explore barriers that might seem obvious to family and friends but not so obvious to the person who is suffering. For me, underneath my denial was the lie—with its manufactured emotions—that the sexual assault I'd experienced was my fault because I'd trusted the perpetrator and let him get so close to me. This lie perpetuated a sense of self-hatred that I couldn't see until I later processed the trauma. My denial also obscured my anger toward God. After all, in my mind, I'd done all the right things, but God had still allowed me to be ambushed.

The two major roadblocks of bitterness and resentment not only hindered my healing but also perpetuated my health issues—migraines, inflammation, depression, and undiagnosed PTSD. Denial was the first barrier I needed to overcome, since it was the barrier that masked all the others.

I'm so thankful that God walked with me through this journey. He never left my side. He called me out of hiding.

He waited for me to lay down my self-protective mechanisms and trust Him as my protector. As I began to see His goodness and love with fresh eyes, my layers of resistance began to fall away. I became able to acknowledge the spiritual and emotional barriers holding me back, and I invited Him to help me overcome them.

In James's case, the primary barriers to receiving help had included his inability to connect with others and his refusal to trust them with his past. When he finally engaged in individual therapy, he began to understand the reasons for the walls he'd erected around his heart. As he continued with therapy, he let down some of those walls and learned to trust again. For more than forty years, he had refused to accept the notion that he may be experiencing PTSD, but the more he uncovered his past traumas, the more his symptoms began to melt away. In his mind, PTSD had seemed like a Pandora's box full of darkness. It took time and hard work, but he finally realized that the light of God's love could overcome that darkness.

● ● ●

God met James in his pain and gave him a sense of empathy he had never known before. James uncovered the source of his suffering, started to be honest with himself about the behaviors he'd been using to survive, and gave them all over to God. In their place, he received God as his protector, comforter, and restorer. He viewed his identity no longer as what he had done or what had been done to him but as that of a precious child redeemed by Christ's sacrificial death. The comfort he received from God became the comfort he desired to share with other combat veterans.

James received healing from his trauma through . . .

Support. James had supportive family members who helped him recognize his need for help. The fallout of trauma is usually manifested first at home and then in other close relationships. After all, family members and close friends are typically the people who know you the best, are around you the most, and can most readily identify your problem areas and changes in behavior. Likewise, they are the ones best suited to offer you love and encouragement.

Courage. James eventually had the courage to face the wounds and haunted memories from his past. A common fear among trauma sufferers is that revisiting painful experiences and emotions will cause them to completely unravel. However, it is vital to explore our trauma, its effects, and the disordered behaviors that have emerged as a result of it. When people can explore their trauma in safe spaces with professional help—and with God's help—they will usually be able to achieve significant progress.

Trust. James let down his protective walls and invited God into the wounded areas of his heart. Many people try to stuff down their traumas and stressors so deeply that they can no longer be bothered by them. But unprocessed emotions will never really go away. Instead, they will continue to build as they become manufactured emotions, leading to further isolation and disordered reasoning. When we try to live in our own strength, we limit God's power in our lives. If we keep our trauma hidden, we accept a life of disordered thoughts and emotions. Even though it was uncomfortable at times, James found comfort in processing his memories instead of avoiding them.

Faith. James invited God to be his protector. This decision eventually empowered him to help others living in a state of denial similar to the one he'd been living in. His former mindset—that he alone had his back and that he needed to be in control at all times—had been exhausting. When he was at last able to let go of control and surrender to God's protection, he finally found peace. No longer did he live in fear, constantly on the lookout for the next looming threat.

• • •

Something shifted in me after I was raped. I understood that I could no longer fight my way out of danger. I felt helpless, stripped of any dignity and worth. What's more, with the exception of my mother, I believed that I could no longer trust anyone close to me. So what did I do? I buried what had happened. I locked it away. I buried the hurt, shame, and defeat. It was another attempt at self-protection, but all it did was open the door for the enemy to wreak havoc in my life and keep my spiritual wounds unaddressed.

Meanwhile, I continued seeking treatment for my TBI. I completed the second surgery necessary to repair my septum, and this time around, I remained in the hospital for monitoring while I recovered from the anesthesia. The surgery itself went well, but my heart rate dipped into the low 30s. It was another setback due to the anesthesia.

After I was finally discharged from the hospital, I tried to return to the treatment center to continue my therapy only to learn that the facility had gone bankrupt and shut down. One step forward, two steps back. I was once again at a loss. I had nowhere to go for treatment and no path toward recovery.

My mother was able to find a treatment center in Texas that specializes in TBIs, and I spent two weeks there in another attempt to get my life back. (I still failed to grasp just how long the process would take.) The staff there discovered that my eyes were not tracking appropriately, and they proposed a series of new therapies. The treatments seemed to really reduce my migraines and significantly improve my vision, but the day I returned to Colorado, I experienced a grand mal seizure. I lost consciousness and awoke to find paramedics in my apartment.

This turned out to be another major setback. I lost most of the gains I had made in Texas. To top it off, the director from my fellowship program called to say that I needed to be 100 percent back to health within a month or else I would lose my spot in the fellowship and would have to reapply and complete the first year all over again.

The silver lining to my Texas treatment experience, though, was being able to meet other veterans with TBIs. It was comforting to learn that I was not alone. The two weeks away from my boyfriend also helped me realize that I no longer wanted him in my life. I was ready to make a change. Meanwhile, my brother in Indiana was about to welcome his first baby. I certainly didn't want to keep my mom from holding her first grandchild, so I encouraged her to return to Indianapolis for a while. Little did I know just how much I would continue to struggle without her—with more seizures, not being able to drive, and not even trusting myself to be alone.

Being alone was a major barrier to my healing. Without my mother around, I was extremely isolated. No one from my fellowship program reached out to me. I had only been in Colorado for about a year prior to my brain injury, so I didn't have a large community of support to lean on, and military protocols prevented me from leaving the state. I entered a time of uncertainty and loneliness. The darkness began to creep in, as did the depression.

REFLECTION

1. Ezekiel 36:26 says, "I will give you a new heart, and a new spirit I will put within you. And I will remove the heart of stone from your flesh and give you a heart of flesh." What comes to mind when you think of God replacing a "heart of stone" with a "heart of flesh"?

2. What might be preventing you from inviting God to soften the hardened places in your heart?

3. In what areas of your life do you feel a sense of detachment or difficulty truly engaging with your emotions?

4. Do you ever find yourself dismissing someone else's suffering, perhaps because you don't think it warrants attention? If so, why do you think that's the case?

CHALLENGE

Think of a scenario in which you tend to dismiss someone else's trauma or stress. Ask God to help you identify anything that might be inhibiting your empathy, and ask Him to give you a heart of compassion for others.

CHAPTER THREE

overcoming psychological barriers to healing

When facing trauma, we're—often unwittingly—compelled to choose a path moving forward. One is to try dealing with our pain ourselves. Denial and avoidance are two ways we might do this. The other path is to acknowledge our wounds and process them, trusting God for healing and transformation.

If the first step to solving a problem is to acknowledge that it exists, the next step is to identify potential barriers to overcoming it. When dealing with trauma, one barrier might be repeated exposure to ongoing traumatic events, wherein the sufferer continues to unravel. Another potential barrier is *cognitive distortion*—accepting lies and misconceptions that prevent a person from seeking help and keep them stuck following a destructive pattern of behavior. These are just a couple of examples of *psychological barriers*.

By the time I met Jill, her life was unraveling from PTSD symptoms that stemmed from repressed childhood trauma. She'd been in therapy for about twenty years, but she still dealt with fear, flashbacks, and nightmares. Even brief or vague memories of her past continued to trigger negative bodily sensations—a rush of adrenaline followed by physical feelings of disgust. Bothered by any woman wearing immodest clothing, she avoided movies, television, and magazines. Her husband's character and loyalty weren't enough to counter her fear that he was lusting after other women or that he might even cheat on her.

Jill had spent many years of her adult life suppressing memories of childhood trauma. One day, however, when she was out jogging, a stranger exposed himself to her. The incident stirred up an intense reaction that finally prompted her to seek clinical help.

As her PTSD symptoms continued, she recognized that her father was a major trigger. A simple phone call from him elicited emotions of dread and fear. When she realized that he was a primary source of her trauma, life as she knew it continued to unravel. She was living in a state of guilt and shame, convinced she was worthless but unable to pinpoint why she felt that way.

A good friend referred her to me, and together Jill and I discovered that her barriers to further healing centered on shame, guilt, and her lack of feeling valued or heard. As we peeled back the layers of her childhood trauma, I learned that her father had frequently sexually assaulted her and her sister. She had tried to block out the memories, but she could not escape the deviance she'd been exposed to.

In our first session, we uncovered the lies she had believed about her identity and value. Her father's assaults had left her feeling unworthy, tainted, and ashamed. She said it was like she was "in the yuck." She believed that sex was the only reason a man would value her, that her husband would leave her if she did not serve that purpose, and that she'd deserved the horrific trauma of her childhood because she was somehow inherently bad. As an adult, Jill felt powerless to view her identity in any other way, and she'd do anything she could to lift herself out of her ongoing shame or feel any sort of worth. She embarked on a campaign to do everything right. She subconsciously tried to make up for her trauma by adopting perfectionistic standards that no one could possibly meet.

In subsequent sessions, we discussed how her low self-esteem stemmed from her history of abuse. However, instead of blaming her father for what he had done to her and her sister, she blamed herself. She developed feelings of self-hatred, somehow convinced that she must have deserved the abuse.

Fear was a major theme throughout her life. She was afraid to make choices, afraid of failure. As we talked, she recognized that her fear was also a defense mechanism. She had used it as her guide in hopes of avoiding more anguish. Subconsciously, she believed that fear was her protector, but in reality, it was destroying her life. She suffered from low self-esteem and feared her husband's pending betrayal because she never felt worthy of anyone's love.

She told me that she'd often turned to God throughout her life—praying and reading His Word—but it had always felt like there was a disconnect. She believed that God could comfort her, but she felt like she couldn't experience that comfort.

She made progress when she started to allow God's love to overcome her fears. She surrendered her need for a defense mechanism. This surrender to a power higher than her own provided relief from the constant hypervigilance and paranoia she experienced on a nearly daily basis.

She realized she needed to trust what God said about her true identity, value, and purpose. She stopped striving to make herself worthy and started resting in Christ's work on the cross—a sacrifice that demonstrated her worth and His love for her.

As she continued dealing with the trauma of her past and invited God to help heal the deepest wounds of her soul, her PTSD symptoms began to dissipate. Her hypervigilance, associated bodily sensations, and low self-esteem melted away. She developed a newfound sense of confidence and a much-improved relationship with her husband.

Jill received healing from her trauma through . . .

Recognition. Jill needed to acknowledge that her childhood trauma was still an issue in her life and that it was holding back her recovery. Many people who experience significant trauma will do almost anything to avoid bringing it up again—and that's if they even admit that it exists. Past trauma, however, will invariably resurface at some point, so the sooner it's dealt with, the less turmoil it will eventually breed.

Confrontation. Jill next needed to expose the falsehoods she'd internalized—misconceptions that perpetuated her feelings of unworthiness, shame, and fear. I've treated many clients who experienced anxiety, fear, or intense sadness but were unable to identify the source of these draining emotions. Whether or not you see a professional therapist, it's vital to find someone you trust who can speak into your life and help you walk through your past trauma.

Faith. Finally, Jill needed to experience the truth in order to overcome the lies she was believing. She claimed to have deep faith in Jesus, as well as intellectual knowledge of her redemption through His death and resurrection. However, due to her ongoing patterns of self-preservation, she was subconsciously blocking the forgiveness, grace, and peace that Christ offers. As we uncovered these lies together and called them out, she let go of them, and they lost the power they'd once wielded in her life. She was at last able to replace them with the truth of God's mercy and love for her.

• • •

Sometimes simply talking about trauma isn't enough. When we first met, a client named Chase was keyed up, rambling, anxious, and restless. Getting him to talk about his pain certainly wasn't a problem, but he was paranoid and irritable. In my professional assessment, he was manic and psychotic. (*Mania* is a mixture of symptoms that includes hyperactivity, racing thoughts and fast speech, increased agitation, a decreased need for sleep, euphoria, grandiosity, impulsivity, and sometimes psychosis, which he demonstrated.)

He'd come across my name while searching for a psychiatrist. He arrived at my office accompanied by his mother, who had come to offer support and provide history. I learned that he had been intermittently manic, psychotic, and depressed for several years. He was constantly in survival mode, blinking in and out of touch with reality. I recommended hospitalization almost immediately.

Why hospitalization? In my office, he was exhibiting paranoia, speaking nonsensically, and acting highly agitated. He wasn't thinking clearly, and it was unclear if he would act out on his agitation and paranoia. He needed to stabilize his moods and receive treatment in a secure environment. Fortunately, he was willing to enter a hospital to receive a higher level of care than I could offer. I could see that he also needed a medication regimen, which I recommended to the admitting psychiatrist.

After about a week in the hospital, he was much more stable. As we continued our sessions, we began to uncover just how much trauma his psychotic and manic episodes were inflicting on him. When he was in the middle of an episode, he would act completely out of character: He'd spend money impulsively, drink excessively, take drugs, and engage in other activities he would later be ashamed of. He'd feel out of control and unable to trust himself. Unlike Jill or James, whose symptoms had stemmed from traumatic events in the past,

Chase's episodes of erratic behavior and impulsivity led to traumatic events in his present.

We spent several sessions dealing with his feelings of shame that stemmed from his behavior during these manic episodes. We discussed the nature of psychosis and mania, and how it is virtually impossible to think rationally or logically in such a state. Chase had a persistent fear of becoming manic and psychotic again. He was terrified of losing control, and I repeatedly reassured him that his new medication regimen was working.

He attended church and some group support meetings, but he couldn't grasp the concept of an ongoing relationship with God. It took time and education—both about his disorders and about the severity of what he'd experienced—plus a significant period of mood stability before he could even begin to feel more secure. His uncontrolled mood disorders were a significant barrier to improving his confidence, relationships, and faith, not to mention gaining and sustaining successful employment. But once he was able to get on the right medications and receive ongoing support, he was able to make progress in his relationships and hold on to a steady job.

Once his bipolar mood swings were under control, we started tackling the fallout from his manic and psychotic episodes, which had led to traumatic events. His erratic behaviors, impulsivity, and paranoia had sometimes led to physical altercations. It wasn't often that he was combative or physically violent toward others, but he had been forcibly removed from places of business on more than one occasion.

His aggressive behaviors were the result of disruptions in his biochemistry, so they were neither planned nor controllable. (Of course, that didn't matter to the people he engaged with in conflict!) Furthermore, not being able to think rationally or process his memories made him more susceptible to developing PTSD after these events. One way he found relief was through specialized psychotherapy, which helped him learn how to distinguish which of his symptoms were trauma related and which were bipolar related.

Left untreated, psychological barriers like mood instability and PTSD can create major disruptions in an individual's life, including unregulated emotions, relational stress, unemployment, and unpredictable behavior. A combination of therapy, support, and the right medications helped Chase overcome these barriers and get his life back.

As we worked together, he made big gains. Not only did he get to start working again, but he also started to experience greater mental clarity and become better able to grasp God's mercy. Christianity finally began to make sense to him, and he recognized Jesus as his Savior and received forgiveness and grace for the first time.

Chase found healing from his trauma through . . .

Hospitalization. Chase needed to receive treatment in a safe, secure environment—one that helped him get his manic episodes and mood swings under control.

Medication. The right medication regimen helped Chase gain mental clarity and, over time, emotional security for the first time in several years.

Stabilization. Once it was evident that Chase's episodes were under control, he was able to gain steady employment, participate in group support, and develop a relationship with Jesus Christ that allowed him to experience God's peace.

•   •   •

The stories of Chase and Jill reminded me of the psychological barriers to healing that I'd faced in my own journey through trauma. In a matter of months, I'd suffered a traumatic brain injury, a sexual assault, and a grand mal seizure. My neurologist put me on anti-seizure medication, and I assured my mom that I would be fine, but I still couldn't drive and was essentially stuck in my apartment. That's when the depression really set in. Whether my depression was due to my unresolved trauma, lack of independence, loneliness, or simply a side effect of the medication, I can't say for sure— all I know is that I fell into an intense period of despondency. Sometimes I just sat and stared into the distance, like my body was filled with lead and I was unable to move.

Meanwhile, the end of my relationship with my boyfriend didn't bring me any peace. I knew it had been the right thing to do, but I had expected God to comfort me and give me peace. Instead, I felt joyless, like I'd just ripped a bandage off my heart. It was also the middle of winter, which didn't help my emotional state. Along with the depression came clouds of helplessness and hopelessness. And more loneliness.

I should have told someone about my depression, but I didn't. Instead, I just wallowed in it, which was exactly the wrong thing to do. To be honest, I had zero motivation to do much of anything. That didn't really matter, though, since I couldn't do much anyway due to my condition.

Depression, at least in my case, made me feel like every positive emotion had fled and numbness had taken over. When my patients suffer from depression, their loved ones are often frustrated by what they see as laziness or disinterest in getting better. These patients are often told that they just need to snap out of it. But they aren't lazy. Depression typically causes an utter lack of energy or drive. Some days it takes everything a person has to simply get out of bed. That's how I felt. I learned that it's hard to truly understand the throes of depression until it envelops you personally.

My former boyfriend kept reaching out, trying to cheer me up. He'd offer to drive me up to the mountains, get food for me, or keep me company. I resisted his offers for about a month, but the depression eventually got to me. The loneliness was too great. I sought comfort in what was comfortable, despite how destructive it was.

I let this man back into my life, partly to spite God for not giving me the comfort and peace I thought I certainly deserved after breaking it off the first time. It wasn't a conscious decision, and I probably didn't realize my motivations at the time, but looking back, that's exactly what I was doing.

In more ways than one, my untreated and ignored depression was a barrier to my relationship with God. It kept me trapped in an unhealthy relationship, and it impeded my healing.

REFLECTION

1. What is the biggest psychological barrier you face?
2. What is an ongoing worry in your life?
3. What is your go-to coping mechanism when you feel insecure, uncomfortable, or stressed? Is it food, drugs, alcohol, affection, or something else?
4. How often do you rely on this coping mechanism, and in what scenario(s) is this most likely to happen?

CHALLENGE

What psychological barriers might prevent you from healing? Identify at least one unhealthy coping mechanism in your life that distracts you from seeking help or receiving comfort from the Lord. Resolve to let go of this behavior or thought process and replace it with a healthy strategy that will draw you closer to healing and to God.

CHAPTER FOUR

overcoming spiritual barriers to healing

God created us to live in community. We crave acceptance and a sense of belonging. Even as children, we want to feel like part of the family or one of the gang on the playground. But the world can be cruel, and life doesn't always work out the way we want. When we are rejected, either through words or actions, the wounds can cut deep.

The result is that sometimes we strive even more for acceptance, attempting to prove that we are worthy of it. Other times we retreat, believing that we are all that we have. This belief—that it's us against the world and no one else is on our side—becomes just another self-protective barrier, a means to insulate us from more rejection and abandonment.

The notion that no one else is trustworthy is a barrier that grows out of fear, and it sentences us to a life of risk mitigation. This barrier seeks to eliminate any potential for betrayal or loneliness. It also blocks us from genuine friendships, love, and freedom. It gets us stuck in a lifestyle of shallow relationships with mere acquaintances where we can't fully know others nor be fully known. In refusing to explore the vulnerable areas of our lives, we only succeed in keeping God and others out. The more we try to prove our worth and find acceptance through word and deed, the more we shut out God's grace. Succeeding on our own is a matter of pride, one that chokes out personal growth and hinders healing.

This method of self-protection is an example of a *spiritual barrier*. What's more, it only works as long as we can master all obstacles on our own. But what happens when we can't outwork, outthink, or overpower the obstacles in our own strength? We eventually crash and burn. We feel helpless, hopeless, and powerless. Then we look for someone or something to distract us from our negative emotions—we look for a way out. And until we turn to a source of strength and grace far greater than ourselves, we are destined to fail.

Many who have what I consider to be an *orphan mentality* face a similar existence: a largely isolated life consumed with striving to earn favor while overcoming rejection. Such a life is devoted to proving others wrong about their tendency toward rejection in order to reach a place of acceptance and belonging. Unfortunately, it's also a constant uphill battle with no end in sight. Countless people struggle with this, seeking to free themselves, find themselves, and save themselves.

Others simply give in to the orphan mentality, accepting

bitterness, resentment, and self-hatred. They find themselves in the same painful situations repeatedly, hoping things will be different each time. This pattern of behavior is called *repetition compulsion syndrome*. For example, someone might seek out the same type of romantic partner over and over, even when those partners are abusive or narcissistic. Those who deal with repetition compulsion syndrome in relationships continue to hope that, at some point, the same old scenario will work out in their favor. It rarely does.

• • •

Scott was an orphan in nearly every sense of the word. His father was murdered when Scott was five years old, and while his mother was alive, throughout his childhood she continually brought abusive men into their home who caused significantly more harm than good. Young Scott watched as his mother was beaten, abandoned, and one time even left for dead.

Needless to say, Scott spent much of his childhood in survival mode. One of his mother's boyfriends tried to drown him in a bathtub. He was sexually molested by a babysitter for several years, but his mom didn't believe that it had happened. He finally found an ally in a neighborhood friend—a connection and lifeline he'd never known before—but that relationship came to an end when the friend took his own life. Eventually, Scott's mother also committed suicide, leaving behind a note that blamed him for her actions.

When he was old enough, he joined the Army. It was his attempt to find purpose and connection, but mostly it was a way to escape the horrors of his life. While he was in the military, however, he faced even more demons and darkness. The specter of suicide continued to haunt him as other friends and fellow soldiers ended their lives. Wherever he turned, he faced abandonment and loss.

Now fending for himself, he used alcohol to escape and numb his emotional pain. He desperately wanted someone to accept him, to love him, and—most of all—to not abandon him. He had never experienced genuine love; all he'd ever known was rejection. As a child, whenever he'd started to depend on someone for love and connection, that person had given up on him. The same pattern continued as an adult, so he found comfort in a bottle.

Like many others with a traumatic past, he got married in an attempt to avoid loneliness, but he never truly opened up his heart to his wife. Their relationship lacked vulnerability and trust. He had hoped that marriage would cure his loneliness, but without a sense of trust, he never put in the work that would have allowed his wife to truly know him.

In fact, the more he tried opening his heart to others, the more anxiety he experienced. *What if they eventually spurn me, just like all the others?* This was the way he thought about God, too. Having never experienced genuine love, he simply couldn't imagine the unfailing love of Christ—unconditional, unwavering, with no strings attached. He believed in the concepts of grace and forgiveness, but not that those concepts applied to him. How could they? Where were the grace and forgiveness from the people who'd been supposed to care for him? The unconditional love of a heavenly Father seemed too good to be true. How could he risk making that leap of faith, only to be rejected again?

So he kept God and everyone else (including his wife) at arm's length. He put his head down and worked hard. He kept busy and kept pushing, working hard at multiple jobs and helping friends out whenever he could—doing whatever it took to shut out the demons from his past. But no matter how much he tried, the grief he was trying to suppress would sometimes rear its ugly head, and a lifetime of guilt and shame would come creeping back. That's when he would start drinking again. And the drinking would only make the dark spiral worse.

Subconsciously, he was caught in a punishing pattern of trying to make up for not being lovable. If something triggered a haunting memory or feeling of unworthiness, alcohol was his self-medication. This pattern is a familiar cycle for many trauma sufferers. Scott pushed himself to exhaustion, to the point where he could no longer sustain all the nonstop striving. He felt like a failure as a husband, son, and father because he could never do enough to make up for what he was feeling. He worked very hard to be the man he thought people wanted him to be, but deep inside he believed he never could.

When I met Scott, he was having big challenges in his marriage. Communication was a huge barrier, and his relationship with his wife was characterized by defensiveness and fear of rejection. He realized that he needed help if he was going to save their marriage. He heard about my Tribe support groups for military veterans and decided to join the meetings.

As we progressed through the weekly sessions, he began sharing snippets of the trauma he'd experienced with the rest of the group. He described trying to keep his trauma at bay by staying distracted with work and helping others, but memories of his past always came flooding back. Those memories convinced him that he was unworthy and wasn't enough.

But as he continued to engage more with others, through the Tribe meetings and in the broader community, he found people who truly cared. He also recognized that alcohol was a major factor in his downward spirals.

He had a lightbulb moment one evening after a Tribe session. As several of us ate dinner together, he opened up to the group about his traumatic past and the resulting shame he felt. That night, as he shared his struggles and his perceived failure as a father, his fellow Tribe members surrounded him, prayed for him, and cried with him. It was the first time he had ever experienced such an outpouring of authentic, unconditional love.

That night was the beginning of a dramatic change for him. He began to see his worth through the eyes of others. He no longer viewed himself as a worthless failure. Instead, he found hope in a new identity. He recognized his value and his need for better self-care. Moreover, he acknowledged the destructive power of alcohol in his life and decided that it needed to go.

Not only did he stop drinking, but he began eating better too. Instead of surrendering to past addictions, he now prays and does breathing exercises when he feels tempted. His suicidal episodes, meanwhile, are a thing of the past. Prayer is a bedrock of his daily life, and his marriage and his relationships with his children have improved dramatically.

Today, he enjoys a peace that he's never experienced before. This has helped open his eyes to the steadfast love of his wife. After all, despite everything they've been through, she has remained by his side. And now that he has turned to God instead of alcohol, their marriage is flourishing.

He has also given up on his fruitless pursuits. No amount of striving could erase his past or the weight of his shame; only God could forgive his mistakes and set him free. He has embraced God's grace and received the love of his heavenly Father. And isn't that—a father's acceptance—what he'd been craving all along? He has invited Christ to heal the hurts and wounds that he tried to suppress for years. Now he is no longer a lonely orphan, but an adopted child of God.

The hymn on pages 69–70, by the poet and hymnist William Cowper, describes the contrast between an orphan's heart and the heart of an adopted child. Someone with an orphan's heart seeks to earn favor and achieve their own righteousness, while an adopted child rests in acceptance, freedom, and unconditional love. This is the transformation that Scott has made over time. For years he lived life as an outsider, always trying to find a way in, until he finally realized that he is already accepted and beloved.

Scott overcame his spiritual barriers and achieved healing by . . .

Reaching out. Scott was barely holding on to his marriage . . . and to his life. He endured crippling loneliness for many years, to the point that he felt like his life didn't really matter. Only as a last resort did he reach out for help, and only then—thanks to an authentic and loving support group—did he begin to see his value. He discovered at last what it means to belong.

Recognizing his weakness. Scott realized that alcohol was a major factor in his downward spirals. Drinking contributed to his suicidal thoughts and compounded his feelings of worthlessness. Getting sober was a vital step on his path to recovery.

Seeing his value. As Scott began to view himself through the eyes of God and others, he no longer believed that he was worthless. This shift in perspective gave him the encouragement he needed to invest in self-care and emotional healing. He allowed God to transform him.

Accepting acceptance. For years, Scott spurned unconditional love—from God and others—in a failing campaign to earn acceptance. As I continued to work with him, he finally gave up trying to make a name for himself and instead learned to rest in God's love and mercy. The Lord's grace, he realized, was indeed sufficient. God was the one parent who would never reject him, abandon him, or betray him. He was finally home where he belonged—in his Father's loving arms.

Overcoming spiritual oppression. Scott grew up with suicide and death all around him, and he spent his adult years running from the shame and grief of his past. But he could never truly escape those moments—typically, fueled by alcohol—when he would give in to the lies that he was better off dead than alive, that suicide was part of his identity, and that he didn't deserve any better. Given that his mom had blamed him for her suicide in the note she'd left behind, he started to believe that he was responsible for tragedy wherever he went. These lies gave the enemy a foothold in his life, which he eventually overcame by calling on God's help with breaking their hold on him. By inviting God to take control, he was liberated from his self-destructive thoughts and behaviors.

Love Constraining to Obedience

*No strength of nature can suffice
    To serve the Lord aright:
And what she has she misapplies,
    For want of clearer light.*

*How long beneath the Law I lay
    In bondage and distress;
I toiled the precept to obey,
    But toiled without success.*

*Then, to abstain from outward sin
    Was more than I could do;
Now, if I feel its power within,
    I feel I hate it too.*

Then all my servile works were done
A righteousness to raise;
Now, freely chosen in the Son,
I freely choose His ways.

'What shall I do,' was then the word
'That I may worthier grow?'
'What shall I render to the Lord?'
Is my inquiry now.

To see the law by Christ fulfilled
And hear His pardoning voice,
Changes a slave into a child,
And duty into choice.

WILLIAM COWPER[1]

• • •

Unlike Scott, I was not an orphan—at least not in the literal sense of the word. I was, however, living life with an orphan mentality. This mentality first surfaced after I was molested by a distant relative when I was five years old. I stuffed that traumatic event down, but the experience initiated a sub-conscious dialogue that convinced me that I was tainted and unworthy of love. No wonder I put such a high value on my virginity—I was trying to redeem a past that was out of my control! Like Scott, I spent years seeking the approval of everyone around me. I wanted them to think that I was good enough. Worthy enough.

But my best efforts always seemed to fall short. I longed to be accepted, but I felt alone. I had a loving family and wonderful parents, but my heart and my past trauma told me that I didn't cut it. I felt compelled to live up to some higher standard that I could never meet. I was a good example of someone with an orphan's heart.

At some point, I decided to change the object of my pursuit. Maybe I could find the affirmation I craved in the form of a husband—that prince who would sweep me off my feet. I dreamed of a love that was palpable, passionate, and unwavering. I wanted someone who would laugh at all my jokes and want nothing more than to spend time with me.

Of course, I was seeking to live up to another virtually impossible standard. Only Jesus Himself could meet my desire for perfection. I continued searching for that wonderful prince, and when he didn't show up, I again concluded that the problem was with me. I was the one who didn't belong. I was the one who was lacking. *Is it that I'm not funny enough, exciting enough, smart enough, pretty enough?* Despite my striving, I could never reach the bar I'd set.

• • •

The person I thought might be my prince ended up hurting me more than anyone. Once my virginity was gone, I was overcome with the desire to redeem the loss. This only reinforced my orphan's heart. I started pursuing every avenue that might make me complete—anything to feel pure again. I tried to mold my boyfriend into the godly husband and spiritual leader I desperately wanted. Most of all, I tried to remove the shame that I felt in my soul.

At that time, I thought I still needed to earn God's approval, to somehow undo what had been done. This led to poor choices on my part as I drifted away from my identity in Christ. My quest to be worthy of a man's love made me lose sight of my true love. Meanwhile, how could I ever feel worthy again when I was so broken by trauma? How could my boyfriend be the man I'd been searching for, the one to unlock my orphan's heart, when he'd acted so terribly? And yet, like so many with an orphan mentality do, I pressed on. I tried to make it all work for weeks, even months, until I eventually came to a defining moment in my life.

My apartment lease was about to expire, and I was still in limbo with the Air Force. I was waiting to see if they would keep me on and assign me to another duty station. My seizures had started to ease up, but I still couldn't read or work, and I still suffered from intractable migraines. Moreover, the setbacks kept coming.

As I slowly weaned myself off my seizure medication, I was involved in another accident. I was riding in the back seat of an SUV on I-70 in Colorado when a deer ran in front of the car. The deer was pulverized on impact, and my body was whipped around in my seat. The driver was able to maneuver the car off to the side of the highway, where it sputtered to a halt, totaled. My mind was foggy, bright stars flooded my vision, and a wave of nausea overwhelmed me.

I climbed out of the car, shaking, and my mind

immediately flashed back to my previous car accidents. The first one had occurred when I'd been hit at a stoplight while in medical school. The second had happened a couple of years later, when I'd been involved in a four-car pileup in Texas during my residency. I'd dealt with chronic pain after that accident, and that's when I'd first developed an aversion to driving or traveling in a car. Every time I got into a vehicle, my body tensed up, subconsciously bracing for another accident. After the highway encounter with the deer, I spent the next two weeks in bed, exhausted. I had to rest my brain yet again.

As I mentioned earlier, I suspected that the Air Force was going to retire me, so I didn't want to commit to another year in an expensive apartment. I made plans to stay with a friend, but the very day I was supposed to move in, those plans fell through. This was after I had broken up with my boyfriend the first time but before I broke up with him for good. In the midst of my scramble to find somewhere to live, lo and behold, he said that I could stay with him, his roommate, two dogs, and a bird. At the time, I knew of no other options.

It took two months of living in his cramped, cluttered apartment, stuck in a bedroom with him and two dogs, before I finally found a way out. A friend of a friend offered up a room in their house. In this house, I found a blessing I'd long been missing: God's Word in my life. My friend read the Bible out loud to me, and it was during these readings that I had my own lightbulb moment.

As I listened to the story of Rachel from Genesis 30—how she said, "Give me children, or I shall die!"—I was struck with a flash of insight. Like Rachel, and like so many others in Scripture, I had treated a potentially good thing as the ultimate thing. I'd wanted a life partner so badly that I had prioritized having one above everything else.

I prayed, asking God to forgive me for making an idol out of my desire for a husband. Then I decided to let go of my boyfriend for good. I was tired of trying to make our relationship work, and I wanted Jesus more than anything else. I finally acknowledged the anger I'd been feeling toward God because He hadn't given me the peace and comfort I'd expected following the initial breakup. In truth, I was simply afraid of the pain that might return. This time, however, I told the Lord, *I don't care how much it hurts again, or if the depression sets in again. I just want You.*

The peace I experienced when I prayed those words? I can't even begin to explain it. Instead of being left in ashes, I felt an all-consuming love envelop me—a love I knew I did not earn or deserve. Comfort and joy and God's goodness filled me like I'd never felt before. I will never forget it. At that moment, I knew what it felt like to "taste and see that the LORD is good" (Psalm 34:8). The true lover of my soul embraced me that night with open arms.

I began to understand the difference between chasing after an imperfect person and inviting Jesus, the Perfect One, to satisfy my deepest longings. He gives Himself to me, and to all His children, completely and without hesitation. For so long I'd wanted to help free others, but I couldn't help them until I'd been set free myself. This was not a lesson I learned quickly, but eventually I did. I wrote about my path toward healing in my journal:

> From the valley of my distress, when my life turned to
>   ashes,
> I looked for a way out. It was as if I were pounding on the
>   walls of a locked tower.
> This locked tower, in reality, was the grip I had to the
>   identity I had formed.
> The mask I'd put on was to help myself feel worthy.
> Under the mask was a scared little girl wanting to be
>   comforted, wanting to be loved, but too far into the
>   darkness of the tower to be found.
> I searched and searched for a way out, but there was no
>   escape.
> I was isolated and alone in the darkness.
> Then trauma after trauma came and broke through
>   the mask that I was hiding behind. The light shined
>   through the wounds in my soul.
> The noise was removed, and I finally heard the voice that
>   had been there all along, saying, "Look up."
> I finally looked up and saw a faint glimmer of light that lit
>   a path in the midst of the darkness.
> As I ascended, I started to feel lighter and loved. The
>   higher I climbed, the more I felt an energy outside of
>   myself fueling me, and I knew I was not alone.

> *The lover of my soul was waiting on me to recognize the*
> *darkness I'd created by hiding behind the masks.*
> *The moment I looked up, I began to realize that Jesus*
> *was there all the time, anticipating the moment that I*
> *would welcome Him in to comfort that lost, sad, and*
> *vulnerable little girl who just wanted to be embraced*
> *by her Daddy.*

I found healing for my "orphan's heart" trauma through . . .

Invitation. The first step toward healing was to cast aside my protective barriers and acknowledge my tendency to cover up traumatic wounds with achievements. The more we try to hide our failings and flaws, the more we prevent God from making us whole. God wants to heal us, but He rarely intervenes without an invitation. The more we try to fix ourselves, the more we interfere with His work in our lives. Revelation 3:20 says, "Behold, I stand at the door and knock. If anyone hears my voice and opens the door, I will come in to him and eat with him, and he with me."

Discovery. I needed to know, to really know, that God was there in the midst of my brokenness. There are times when we do not feel God's presence. Indeed, there are times when all we feel is despair and a sense of failure. These are the moments when we need to look to Jesus more than ever. It helped to remind myself of a love so powerful that it brought Jesus to the cross. He gave up His earthly life to give me everlasting life. I am His beloved, and only He can make me whole.

Humility. Trying to prove my worth with achievements

didn't work. That is the tendency of an orphan's heart, but it has never worked. It's just another form of pride. The better path, I learned, was to humble myself, to recognize my need for God's grace. God loves me and accepts me just as I am. I am completely unable to earn His favor. I didn't recognize the orphaned life I was living until the walls I'd built to hide my imperfections came crashing down. This was my turning point. My achievements were reduced to rubble, and I was forced to face my vulnerability. My sin. This is where I found my Savior. All along He'd held me through the suffering, and now He felt closer than ever. None of my achievements mattered to Him; He wanted only my heart.

Commitment. I committed to being always on my guard, watching out for those moments when I find myself reverting to the orphan mentality of striving and proving. As flawed humans, we all live in the constant tension between God's ways and our own desires. We are inundated with lies and temptations that try to lure us to embrace the cares of this world. Following God involves reminding ourselves every day that we cannot prove our worth. Christ's sacrifice is the only demonstration of our value that we will ever need.

REFLECTION

1. What is a significant spiritual barrier in your life?
2. Have you ever felt like God has intentionally withheld something that you desired or felt you needed or deserved?

3. Have you ever felt like you've had to pay for or bear the weight of what you've done wrong?

4. Have you ever felt unable to receive forgiveness? If so, what does that tell you about your perception of God?

CHALLENGE

Identify some times in your life when you've been vulnerable, felt weak, or succumbed to temptation. Did you try to deny your vulnerabilities, seek to cover up your pain, or attempt to push through on your own? Ask God to forgive you and to help you come directly to Him in times of need. Remember that in our weakness He offers us His strength. From now on, whenever you feel weak, go to Him right away.

overcoming relational barriers to healing

Sometimes when people experience hurt, betrayal, rejection, or the loss of a loved one, they often respond with avoidance or isolation. Other times, it's just the opposite—they act out in order to try to get the attention they've lacked in the past. Either response makes integrating into one's community more difficult, just as negative behaviors make it harder to find necessary support. In other words, trauma often makes the hurdles to forming healthy relationships even higher by preventing those who suffer from being fully integrated in society and the body of Christ.

I refer to these hurdles as *relational barriers*. Codependent relationships are one such barrier. These often occur when someone who's suffered trauma latches onto another person and puts them on a pedestal, expecting that person to meet all of his or her needs. Another such barrier is hypervigilance, which can develop when someone is constantly on the lookout for a looming threat or feeling like danger is always lurking just around the corner. People can be hypervigilant toward relationships as well as society at large. When people constantly expect others to fail them, betray them, or reject them, they have a difficult time trusting anyone. Why would you ever display even a hint of vulnerability if you are always expecting the worst?

• • •

Shelby was working as a first responder when she signed up for a Tribe group that met at the church she attended. She said very little during the first few meetings but slowly began to open up as the program progressed. She shared with the group that she was going through a divorce from her high school sweetheart after discovering that he was cheating on her. Not only did her husband have no intention of ending the affair, but he'd announced that he was leaving her for the other woman. She also told the group about how her father had died when she was a child, a point at which her young life changed had forever.

When the eight-week Tribe session ended, she inquired about receiving additional help through individual therapy. In the individual sessions that followed, she told me that one of her barriers to healing was alcohol. Her drinking problem began years ago at age thirteen when her father was first diagnosed with cancer. Alcohol became her coping mechanism—a habit that persisted for many years.

Her father passed away less than a year after he was diagnosed, leaving her devastated. She went from being daddy's little angel to receiving little to no comfort from other family members. She generally felt dismissed and forgotten, essentially unheard by the rest of her family.

The only attention she did receive came from those in her social circle. They were impressed by how much alcohol she could down, so she embraced a new identity as a party girl. Her ability to consume liquor became a badge of honor. She was convinced that she was more fun to be around when she was drinking. The further she drifted from her family, the more time she spent with her high school boyfriend. With no father figure in her life, this young man became her anchor. He did everything with her and supported her when her family didn't. His firm commitment to her in high school made his later betrayal that much more devastating.

After her husband left her, she experienced a degree of anger she hadn't felt since her father's passing. She was angry at God over her dad's death; she was angry at her family for not supporting her; she was angry at the man she had loved so much; she was angry at herself for not getting over all of it. As we continued with her treatment, we worked through her anger, her alcohol use, and the process of forgiving both her ex-husband and her family.

Shelby, however, denied that her drinking was much of a problem. Many people will continue in a state of denial until they have no other choice—until the realities of life force them to consider the seriousness of their situation.

In her case, she refused to acknowledge the impact of her alcohol consumption until she was charged with driving while under the influence. This became her lightbulb moment, although probably not in the way she would have liked. She lost not only her job as a result but also the house she had recently purchased. At first, she responded with more anger—anger at her ex-husband, anger at God, anger at herself. But hitting rock bottom led her to study the Bible more. And the more she poured herself into Christian teachings, the more she was able to let God soothe her anger.

For years, she had used alcohol to numb her feelings, but now she was determined to deal with her emotions and memories head-on. She eventually realized that she could both have fun and *be* fun without drinking. For the first time in years, she experienced her emotions free from the haze of alcohol. She felt empowered, more confident, and healthier overall. When she let go of the anger she felt toward her ex-husband, it was like a great weight was lifted from her chest. Most importantly, she let go of her anger toward God. She realized that He was for her and not against her and that He had actually been with her, loving her, all along.

• • •

For years, Shelby believed that drinking helped her integrate into her community—that it was actually a benefit to her relationships. She felt like she needed this community.

Therefore, her alcohol consumption was a major barrier to healing. Once that barrier was removed, she was able to deal with the whirlwind of emotions stirred up by the loss of her father, her husband, and her career. She learned to distinguish between her true friends—the ones who wanted the best for her—and her party friends. She established boundaries in her relationships to help preserve her health and keep herself from situations where she would succumb to temptation.

She continued to improve as she found supportive people who cared about her. She gave up her party-girl persona and adopted a new identity as a beloved daughter of God. She reconnected with her family and shared how she'd been hurt by their actions following her father's death. Her family members sincerely apologized, and Shelby was able to achieve reconciliation and improved relationships with them. She eventually obtained an even better job than the one she'd had before, and she remains sober to this day.

Shelby overcame her relational barriers and achieved healing by . . .

Developing boundaries. Clear and consistent boundaries are vital to building healthy relationships. Since alcohol had been a major barrier for Shelby, developing healthy boundaries meant she needed to associate with people who didn't encourage her to drink—people who respected her needs and concerns. (A great resource on the importance of defining and enforcing these kinds of borders is the book *Boundaries* by psychologists Henry Cloud and John Townsend.)

Feeling heard. It is important to know that others hear us, see us, and accept us. Shelby needed encouragement in her ongoing fight for wholeness. She needed to know that she was an integral part of her community and society and that her voice mattered. When people feel unheard, they either shrink further into isolation or end up fighting for others' attention, often in maladaptive ways.

Finding a safe space. Everyone needs to decompress at some point, and that usually requires a safe space to vent freely. For those with a history of trauma, feeling trapped typically induces an intense drive to fight, flee, or freeze. Feeling trapped is a reminder of previous trauma—moments when escape had been impossible and the subconscious desire to survive had kicked in. At these moments, executive functioning, planning, clarity, and decision-making skills go out the window. Shelby found a safe space in the Tribe group, where she could talk about her relationship troubles as well as her alcohol use. Before she opened up to the group, she didn't realize just how often she was turning to alcohol as a means of escape. Once she learned to share her struggles at Tribe, she was also able to find quiet, safe spaces at home where she could reduce the noise, refocus, and connect with God.

Pursuing purpose. Shelby needed to know that God was for her and had a purpose and plan for her specifically. Most of us want to know that we are valued in our communities and are appreciated members of society, and all the more in the scope of eternity. Shelby needed a reason to wake up in the morning, to work hard, to do what was right. Once she found that reason in God, it was no longer devastating when people failed her or her plans went awry. She found a greater purpose and mission. When people recognize the goodness of God and the truth that He delights in them, their need for attention and affirmation loses its power and fades into the background.

Forgiving and being forgiven. Achieving reconciliation with God and others is key to maintaining the health of our souls. The more we compare the depth of our own darkness to the unconditional forgiveness that God offers, the more we open up to forgiving others. Forgiveness is like freedom from debt. Each time someone wrongs us, they accrue debt toward us. We can choose to hold them to that debt or let it go. We hold them responsible for it by withholding things like love, attention, acceptance, respect, and appreciation. The longer we withhold forgiveness, the greater the weight of the debt, as well as the risk that the debt will eventually bury us in resentment and bitterness. Shelby needed to forgive her family members, including some who had no idea what they'd done, in order to find freedom. She needed to let go of her past in order to demonstrate God's grace to others.

• • •

In my own experience with trauma after my TBI, I faced numerous social and relational barriers, none more disheartening than loneliness. I was a major in the United States Air Force, but my commanding officer was stationed halfway across the country. I had no other military members around me nor any major medical installation nearby. I had no visitors from my fellowship, and my family members all lived in different states. Moreover, I had just started attending a new church the weekend before my hiking accident, and I hadn't made any new friends yet. My mother's visits to Colorado were my only source of company.

My relational barriers only increased after my boyfriend assaulted me and I (for a time) ended the relationship. I started to mistrust everyone. It didn't matter whether I'd known people for years or a matter of moments—I became convinced that each and every one of them had an ulterior motive, that no one could be trusted. I was so vulnerable, in fact, that I felt like I could no longer even trust myself.

As my isolation deepened, I had little desire to make new friends. No one was getting close to me. No one. So why bother? I thought I was protecting myself, but my behavior actually made things worse, perpetuating my pain and loneliness.

This is why therapists are often unable to treat themselves. I couldn't recognize that my own relational barriers (or other barriers) existed, nor was I willing to examine my trauma and hurt until much later. My embrace of isolation, distrust, and avoidance was actually quite typical. That's what trauma sufferers do. Until we understand what we're facing, until we learn how to get better, we spend our days simply trying to survive.

But I wasn't about to give up. If I had any hope of addressing my relational barriers to healing, I first needed to come to grips with my trauma and with the patterns of behavior that were now running my life. My PTSD diagnosis was just the beginning. After consulting with several providers, I decided to undergo cognitive processing therapy (CPT) through the Department of Veterans Affairs.

CPT helps people with PTSD symptoms work through the distorted thinking that often manifests itself after a traumatic experience. In my case, a therapist walked me through my thoughts and feelings and helped me recognize them as distortions. For example, one of my distortions was that I was the one to blame for being raped. Somewhere deep down, I believed that I should have been able to foresee the sexual assault and that I could have avoided it. When my therapist helped me see that I couldn't have predicted or prevented my assault, it enabled me to redirect my anger and stop blaming myself.

I'd also been engaging in a form of control that was doomed to fail: As long as I could point to something I'd done wrong in the past, I assumed that I could prevent additional trauma from happening in the future. This was illogical, of course. No amount of convoluted thinking could protect me from future trauma, even if I vaguely recognized some similarities between current experiences and previous ones. I was only deceiving myself. This was just one more maladaptive coping mechanism.

After several weeks of CPT, I found a Christian therapist who helped me recognize that I needed to rely on God as my protector and to trust Him with my future. I learned to stop fearing the looming specter of potentially traumatic events. Rather, I began viewing those future experiences as things

God could use to sharpen and transform me. As I learned to give up my need for control, trusting that God's love and wisdom would guide me, my relational barriers began to crumble. I began reaching out to more people, and I developed new friendships. I was no longer afraid of letting people see my vulnerabilities.

As I began sharing my story with others, my fears of betrayal, rejection, and abandonment lost their grip in the light of God's protection. I was living life without a mask, no longer trying to be the person others wanted me to be. It was so liberating that I wanted to share the freedom I'd found with others.

There is great power when people come together as a community focused on healing, especially when such a group relies on God as their foundation. It was the community I experienced that led me to start a series of support groups, which would eventually come to be known as Advancing Warriors International, to help others achieve recovery, growth, and empowerment. No one should ever face suffering alone. This is what the body of Christ is meant to do.

REFLECTION

1. What is a major relational barrier that you face? How does the healthy need for community often get corrupted to become a barrier to healing?

2. What do you think might be causing or reinforcing that relational barrier? How can you begin to remove the strongholds connected with it?

3. In what relationships or experiences have you found yourself resentful, bitter, or unable to forgive others or yourself?

CHALLENGE

Commit to resolving any grievances you have with the people in your life, whether they hurt you or you hurt them. The simplest way to begin is by going to someone you have wronged and asking for forgiveness. This doesn't mean that you condone what either one of you did, but it releases the debt that's been accrued due to the transgression.

CHAPTER SIX

overcoming societal
barriers to healing

Do not be conformed to this world, but be transformed by the
renewal of your mind, that by testing you may discern what is
the will of God, what is good and acceptable and perfect.

ROMANS 12:2

Christians believe that this world is not our home (John 15:19), yet here we are. Living. In this world.

While we're here, we're called by God to reflect His message of love and forgiveness to others. The trouble is that there are plenty of distractions that keep others from receiving that message—lack of understanding, troubles and persecution, the worries of life, the deceptive lure of wealth. Jesus spoke of similar distractions in Matthew 13, in the passage known as the Parable of the Sower. In this parable, a farmer plants seeds in a variety of conditions—on a path, in rich soil, in rocky soil, and among thorns. Jesus explains that these different types of soil are like the different types of people who hear God's Word. Seeds of love and truth can be suppressed or welcomed depending on the heart conditions of those who hear God's message.

Societal barriers to healing are barriers from one's surrounding world, such as problems related to access to medical care or the cost of insurance or medications. One such barrier is the time it takes to receive care. Patients sometimes sit for hours in a waiting room or wait for months just to see a provider. And once they secure an appointment, one can only hope that the provider is a compassionate advocate for the patient, someone who takes the time necessary to give the right care. It's easy to feel like a number, boxed and labeled according to your prescribed treatment. For trauma sufferers, another big part of the struggle is finding a therapist who shares your faith and values.

There is a prevailing negative attitude among people who develop PTSD symptoms. This mindset fosters bitterness and resentment toward those who have wronged us, which lead to still more barriers. We can even harbor bitterness and resentment toward ourselves, bringing on more health issues and additional stress. The mere process of seeking treatment can itself be an additional barrier, something anyone who's worked with hospitals or mental-health clinics can attest to. When you are struggling with the effects of trauma, navigating the healthcare system can feel overwhelming.

There are surely days when it feels easier to give up than to fight through the barriers, especially if no one is advocating for you or encouraging you to stay in the struggle. Dealing with phone calls, procedures, and paperwork, not to mention all the waiting, is enough to make someone who is even the least bit avoidant give in. Add in the nature of how trauma affects many people (typically encouraging avoidance), and surrender can seem like the easy way out.

This is why it's so vital to have a supportive community around you—people who share your beliefs and genuinely care about your well-being. Most of all, it's vital to draw comfort and strength from the Lord, who loves you. We can either conform to this world and limit ourselves to human wisdom or ask God to transform us and renew our minds. The latter option offers the hope of peace through our suffering and provides a steadfast anchor during the storms of life.

• • •

I never fully grasped what it takes to navigate the healthcare system where I live until I had to do it for myself. Sure, I was familiar with many common complaints from a physician's perspective: problems with insurance, limited time with patients, the high cost of medications and treatment. But my eyes were truly opened to the challenges when I became the patient. I saw what folks on the other side experienced—and it was not what I expected.

So much of the process felt like a guessing game—and not the fun kind. I couldn't find any further help, so I had to research my own treatments. Some people even put the blame back on me for not recovering quickly enough. They dismissed my issues and invalidated my concerns.

"It's all in your head," I was told. "You should have

recovered by now." And then this gem: "At least you didn't lose a limb."

This was in the hospital where I was sent on military orders to seek treatment. *Shouldn't they be able to help?* After my second concussion, one civilian psychologist told me that I should have been feeling better within three months. Any lingering issues, he said, were probably due to a mental disorder.

It was extremely frustrating to endure, but I'd heard tales far worse than mine from other patients. And as a veteran I did have access to more treatment options than most civilians, thanks in part to connections among my fellow vets. But finding the right programs took a lot of time and research. And with no clear answers on which specific treatments could help me, I tried all sorts of things, from neurology consultations to hyperbaric oxygen therapy, from Botox for migraines to countless medications.

Thankfully, I had my mother by my side, someone with more than thirty years of experience as a newborn intensive care nurse. Mom coordinated my appointments, drove me when I was unable to drive myself, and helped keep me on track with prescriptions and therapy. She, too, faced a lot of stress and turmoil. She was tired of seeing me suffer. She just wanted her daughter back.

When dealing with traumatic brain injuries in which the patient can barely function, societal barriers are nearly impossible to navigate alone. Frustration sets in easily, and then it settles in. The waiting times, constant phone calls, and need to schedule appointments are not conducive to a smooth recovery. The thought of handling it all by myself, without support, seemed overwhelming.

My mother probably endured more than I even realized. I was blessed to have a willing caregiver when many trauma sufferers have no one, but even this blessing came with a downside: No one had prepared me for the experience of being utterly dependent on someone else or for how it would feel to lose my independence after being self-sufficient for so long. After all, I was the one who had found purpose in treating others. What was my purpose now?

What am I good for?

• • •

Another big societal barrier to healing is the rise of personal technology, and with it the bottomless amounts of social media that users consume.

I'm not saying that all technology is bad, or even that personal technology is all bad. Science and modern technology have given us nearly instant access to virtually unlimited information, goods, and services. Technology helps save lives and solve complex problems. It allows us to gather virtually with people across the globe.

But, like many modern advances, personal technology also has a dark side. It is a constant source of extraneous noise. Face-to-face interaction has significantly decreased as people have come to spend hours on their phones and other devices, checking messages or scrolling through social media. Now that we're used to the immediate gratification of social media, conventional human interaction can seem dull by comparison. This, in turn, has led to neglected relationships and disconnected societies.

How many text conversations have gone awry due to the elimination of nonverbal communication? Without in-person interaction, the ability to show and feel love is compromised. Words alone are often not enough. The onset of the COVID-19 virus only accelerated this trend. The sudden need to wear masks due to the coronavirus pandemic inhibited our nonverbal communication by limiting our ability to pick up on everyday facial cues. With this change, people used to relying on reading facial expressions, on seeing smiles and friendly looks, saw a marked rise in feelings of anxiety.

Not only are we interacting less, but personal technology also gives us another excuse to actually avoid other people. One of the leading factors behind this disconnect is the easy access to pornography.

Pornography is a major barrier to healing in relationships. It interferes with healthy attachment, vulnerability, transparency, and just plain connection with others. It is also highly addictive because it stimulates reward pathways in the brain and feelings of gratification in the body. According to a study reported at the PsychCentral website—a resource created and reviewed by mental-health professionals—about 40 million Americans say that they regularly visit porn sites, 35 percent of all downloads from the internet are pornographic, and 25 percent of search engine requests are related to sex.[1]

The sheer amount of pornography freely available on the internet, combined with the ability to access it whenever and wherever people want, mean that untold numbers of men in the United States view porn at least once a month. And it's not just online. Pornographic or nearly pornographic images are all around us, being used to sell just about everything. Advertising that would have been considered pornographic twenty years ago is now seen by most as no big deal.

Pornography exploits the people involved in creating it as well as the consumer. It degrades and objectifies participants, depicting sex as transactional rather than as part of the beautiful union between husband and wife that God intended. God's Word tells us that looking for sexual fulfillment or satisfaction outside of His design is adulterous. Some may view this perspective as harsh or extreme, but Jesus said that anyone who looks at a woman lustfully "has already committed adultery with her in his heart" (Matthew 5:28).

Porn use is extremely addictive, and it can lower the user's self-esteem to the point that he or she no longer feels desirable. It destroys relationships. After all, who can compete with a sexual fantasy world that only exists on a screen? Until its users recognize the damage that porn can cause, they will likely never take the steps necessary to escape its grip.

● ● ●

By 2017, after nearly two years of multiple concussions, vision problems, and almost constant migraines, I still couldn't work. Even more disheartening, there was no path to healing in sight. The Air Force had shuffled me from one commander to another, and I was in the midst of a medical board review to determine whether or not they would retire me. For most of this time, I was in the dark. I had no idea when the medical board would make their decision, nor did I have any indication of what the decision might be.

I decided to buy a house while I still had a salary. I figured that it was better to invest my money in property than to spend it on rent. And then, no matter whether the Air Force kept me or retired me, I would at least have a place to stay, and I could always rent it out if I improved and the Air Force stationed me somewhere else.

What I didn't realize at the time was how much work it is to own a house. Some friends of mine lived in the lower level of the house I bought, and they were able to help me with some of the maintenance, but my migraines weren't letting up, and I didn't know how long the medical board review would last. I told my latest commander that I still couldn't read and that I had basically run out of treatment options at my current base. Fortunately, he was able to attach me to a medical unit in nearby Colorado Springs, where I would have access to some TBI specialists.

The neurologist and psychiatrist I met with suggested sending me to a major military hospital on the East Coast. There I would have access to even more specialists, and this gave me hope that I would find some answers. I eagerly agreed, and the social worker who made the arrangements told my mother that she should go along. At this point I could barely read a restaurant menu without triggering nausea. I was truly desperate.

When I arrived at the hospital, however, I discovered that my assigned floor was a combined treatment center for traumatic brain injuries and behavioral health. Given that it was a behavioral health unit, my freedom was severely restricted. I'd had no clue what I was in for, and I had little choice but to submit to the hospital staff as they took inventory of my personal belongings. Not only did they take away my razor, but I couldn't even have a mirror of any kind.

I spent my first week there taking a variety of psychological, personality, and mood tests. Since the tests required reading and concentration, they only made my symptoms worse. I expressed concerns about the lighting and noise, but they were largely ignored, and my pleas went unaddressed for several days. Then the first batch of my test results turned out to be inaccurate. This made the staff realize that the testing environment was detrimental to my ability to function and my headaches had skewed the results. To make matters worse, the lights in my room flickered, which exacerbated my discomfort. They were never repaired in the three weeks I was there.

I wasn't allowed to leave the floor unless my mother escorted me. Day passes were difficult to get and usually required groveling. Once I wanted a four-hour pass to visit some friends in the area whom I hadn't seen in years. They invited me to a birthday party that started at 8:00 p.m., but the staff was adamant that I had to be back at the hospital by 9:00. Some of them behaved more like prison guards than nurses. I understand that they felt they needed to do this because they worked in a behavioral health unit, but if I somehow did have a psychiatric diagnosis, they did little to make me feel better about myself!

In fact, to the contrary, one of the nurses told me that my symptoms were all in my head. In her opinion, mine was a simple case of mind over matter. But if that was the case, none of them ever suggested any therapy in that regard. I simply spent lots of time sitting in a hospital bed, bored to death.

Thank goodness for my internal medicine consultation, which revealed iron deficiency anemia. That would account for some of my fatigue, dizziness, headaches, and restlessness at night. Once I received this information, I saw a neuro-optometrist, who diagnosed a dysfunction with my visual tracking system. My eyes weren't coordinating correctly, which was what was making it so difficult to read. This condition is apparently common with TBIs but is often overlooked. My problems focusing also contributed to my migraines. The prescribed treatment was at least six months of vision therapy.

My time at the facility was unpleasant, but at least I had some answers. I could treat my anemia with diet changes and supplements, and I had a plan to address my vision problems. It felt like I was finally on the road to getting my life back. My discharge paperwork, however, revealed that the hospital staff was unsympathetic to my concerns. They suggested that I was overreporting my symptoms and even attributed some of my issues to possible substance abuse. The summary never mentioned my anemia diagnosis or any of the findings regarding my vision.

But with answers in hand, I was just glad to be leaving.

• • •

John is a military veteran and trauma sufferer who had done a lot of work in individual and group therapy before I ever met him. He told me he was interested in helping facilitate one of my Tribe groups for veterans, and he shared his story with me over a cup of coffee. He described his struggles with pornography and how he'd used it to distract himself from the negative effects of his past trauma and heartache.

"My struggle with pornography started with a broken heart," he said. We talked about how it's often the case that people who struggle with addiction have been through a traumatic loss and chosen to turn to the wrong solutions to ease their pain. "That's what happened to me," he affirmed.

He agreed to write down some notes from his journey through trauma, addiction, and redemption, and with his permission, I share a portion of his story here:

I was ten years into an Army career as a helicopter instructor pilot and five years into my marriage. When I was given orders to move to another duty station, my wife informed me that she was not coming with me. She refused to leave Alabama, and she said that she was done with our marriage. We had two children, and I was devastated.

I became angry and turned to pornography to ease my pain. A year later, my wife changed her mind and moved to Tennessee to be with me, but it was too late. I was hooked. She soon regretted leaving Alabama after she saw the power of my addiction. She could no longer trust me, and our children were witnesses to a slow-motion train wreck of a marriage.

I saw the devastation that my addiction caused, and I ended up abstaining for a while. I was working as a Black Hawk helicopter instructor pilot for the National Guard, and I really loved my job and Tennessee. Our kids were now in school, and things seemed to be getting better . . .

But things wouldn't be getting better anytime soon. The moment John watched two airliners fly into the World Trade Center towers, he knew his life as a military aviator would soon change. He was eventually deployed to northern Iraq, where he was involved in an airborne collision with another helicopter. The two pilots in the other copter, both from South Carolina, did not live. All eight people aboard John's aircraft survived.

The National Guard opened a high-profile investigation, and all eyes were on John as the senior pilot who had survived. He had very little time to process the loss. The accident investigation was difficult, but he was back in the cockpit less than a month later. While his commander tried to get him sent back to the States, John's children were dealing with trauma of their own. His fifth-grade son, for example, had to change schools following the stress of his father's deployment and accident.

After fifteen months away from home, John finally returned to a hero's welcome. But he still couldn't get thoughts of the crash out of his mind:

A deep hatred grew inside me for the leaders involved in the crash investigation. I was emotionally numb, completely detached from my family, and suffering from survivor's remorse. I could not stop thinking about the families of the pilots from South Carolina.

My relationship with my wife became worse when she was diagnosed with breast cancer and I showed no emotional response whatsoever. I was looking at pornography again as a way to ease my pain, which deepened my feelings of detachment and fed my anger. A year later, my wife was done [with me] and moved out with the kids. I tried counseling, but I never quit blaming everyone else for my issues. I now realize that if you bring your pride and blame [of others] into counseling, it will never work.

My wife and I stayed married, but her trust in me was gone. Still dealing with survivor's remorse and embroiled with anger, I developed [anger] issues to the point that my children and wife were afraid of me. My solution was to volunteer for another deployment.

He returned to northern Iraq in 2009, as the war was winding down. He figured that his family was better off without him, so he didn't care if he returned or not. He continued to look at porn when he wasn't flying, and his anger issues got worse:

> I always found someone new to hate. Then I went through another traumatic experience: In February 2010, as our National Guard unit was heading to Kuwait to go home, there was an aircraft crash with two fatalities. I was tasked with transporting the bodies, and I had known one of the pilots since she'd been a teenager hanging out at our flight facility. On that very flight, I started having flashbacks of my crash. The other pilot took over the aircraft, and we never said a word. Once again my pain turned into anger, and my anger turned me to pornography.
>
> I returned home just in time for my daughter's high school graduation. My level of detachment was immediately apparent to my wife, as was the pornography use. My relationships at work were deteriorating, and I was in constant conflict with my leadership. In 2012, my wife informed me that an officer I worked with was coming to her workplace to discuss my mental-health and marital issues. I started thinking about assaulting this man, who worked in the same building as me. Finally, out of frustration, I called a suicide hotline because I was afraid I would

actually act on this impulse. I went to a government-provided psychologist for about three months. At the end of our therapy sessions, she said that it might help for my wife to watch the pornography with me to help our marriage. I knew this was a dead end for me, and I sought out a Christian therapist.

I started going to a Christian counselor for my addiction to pornography. He explained to me that the pornography was a symptom of a deeper problem and that I could begin to break its power over me by confessing it as sin and asking God to forgive me.

And that is what happened. It took some time, but I eventually lost my desire to look at it. I started going to Celebrate Recovery, a Christ-centered recovery group, and found healing and support. I went to my wife and told her that I had freedom from pornography, but of course she didn't believe me. There was no trust between us anymore, and as soon as my son left for college, she moved out and filed for divorce. She said she was afraid to be alone with me.

It's often very difficult for people to overcome a powerful addiction like pornography. Healing eluded John, too, until he was able to identify and address the underlying trauma that had perpetuated his addiction, at which point the addiction lost much of its power over him. It sounds too easy to pray and receive healing, but John did more than just pray. He began by acknowledging the weight of his sin—the extent of the depravity—and surrendering it to the Lord. He asked God to reveal the source of his anger—anger that had driven him to pornography as a way to seek comfort and avoid emotional pain.

He committed to dealing with his trauma and coming to terms with his resentment, bitterness, and moral failings. This was easier said than done, of course, since receiving forgiveness is sometimes the hardest part. But as he humbled himself, he was able to both receive forgiveness and forgive others. Many people aren't willing to invest in the deep work that he did. Addicts also need ongoing accountability and support, which he found and maintains to this day. His greatest weapon against addiction, however, has been confession and repentance.

People who are trying to overcome addiction often fail to recognize the power of genuine repentance. Some are concerned with avoiding getting caught and having to face the consequences, while others try to overcome their addictions in their own strength. Others get caught up in punishing themselves and thus minimize God's forgiveness. The better we're able to experience God's love and use that as our motivation, the more our addictions lose their power.

The enemy, however, tells us that our addictions are too strong, that they're too tough to shake, that even God's grace isn't enough to set us free. The result is an unwitting commitment to keeping our addictions unexamined and unaddressed. This, of course, is a recipe for failure. We have to examine them! How can anyone ever heal until they acknowledge their need for healing? How can we "fix" an addiction without addressing what drove us to it in the first place?

Too often people return to their addictions as a source of comfort. In so doing, they end up diminishing the true source of comfort that they've needed all along—God's love. John learned that looking at pornography was his attempt to fill a void that only the Lord could satisfy. His porn habit was, in a way, preventing him from receiving God's comfort. As he identified the triggers of his addiction, he learned that his own strength isn't enough but that God's power is.

He retired from the military due to back problems in 2014, around the same time he was identified as having an adjustment disorder. Once that was in his medical records, his flying career was over. His thousands of hours of flight time were meaningless. By the time he left the National Guard in 2014, he was flagged as a dangerous person. He required an escort just to enter the building where he filed his retirement paperwork.

He wanted to get away and clear his head, so he spent the summer of 2015 walking the Colorado Trail, a 500-mile hike from Denver to Durango.

It turned into a 500-mile prayer walk. I asked God why He hated me so much, and His answer was always "I don't hate you. *You* hate you." So I wrestled with Him in prayer for two months. I blamed everyone for my problems, including Him. I realized that I had made my anger an idol to help keep people away and to insulate myself from more pain.

Through the beautiful scenery and physical activity of hiking in the Rocky Mountains, God showed me that being angry was a choice and that it grieved the Holy Spirit, who has been given to us to be a counselor. Ephesians 4:30-32 says: "Do not grieve the Holy Spirit of God, by whom you were sealed for the day of redemption. Let all bitterness and wrath and anger and clamor and slander be put away from you, along with all malice. Be kind to one another, tenderhearted, forgiving one another, as God in Christ forgave you."

I asked my children and my ex-wife to forgive me. My children did, but it took my ex-wife a few years to get there. I made a list of people I needed to forgive and people I needed to ask for forgiveness. I started the process of reconciliation that Jesus calls us to. I had truly humbling conversations with people I'd hurt. I have learned to feed my relationship with the Holy Spirit through prayer, study of the Word, worship, and fellowship, and I've received the fruit of the Spirit: love, joy, peace, patience, kindness, goodness, faithfulness, gentleness, and self-control (Galatians 5:22-23). These are the tools we need to build relationships. Without them, we are essentially relationally dysfunctional.

When John first embarked on his hike across Colorado, he didn't anticipate that he would end up confronting the issues he had long refused to face. But during those hours alone on the trail, he had his own sort of lightbulb moment. He began to consider the devastation his unprocessed trauma, resentment, and bitterness had caused and how this unprocessed trauma had led him toward pornography as a coping mechanism. He recognized that his unresolved anger was hindering the influence of God's Spirit in his life. This is when he was finally able to surrender his anger and embark on a path to healing by forgiving others and receiving forgiveness himself.

He had come so far and overcome so much trauma that he wanted to help others achieve the same freedom he'd found. He'd learned the hard way that pornography is a societal barrier that steals joy, prevents healing, and destroys relationships and that its effects cannot be brushed aside or easily dismissed. He'd been able to overcome the influence of pornography through the power of Jesus Christ, and he now facilitates Tribe group sessions to help encourage others. After experiencing God's love and forgiveness for himself, he now wants to spread it to everyone he comes in contact with.

John overcame his societal barriers and found healing by . . .

Acknowledging his trauma. He also recognized his very real anger toward God for allowing it to happen. Many Christians feel guilty about expressing their negative emotions to the Lord, but He can handle them. Through the

Psalms, David poured his heart out to God. He often blamed God for his troubles, yet he was described in Scripture as "a man after [God's] own heart" (1 Samuel 13:14). God wants us to approach Him as we are, not hiding behind stoic masks and pretending everything is fine. He wants us to be genuine and honest about our feelings, an attitude that will help us be genuine and honest with ourselves.

Confessing his addiction. John eventually recognized the destructive power of pornography, and that he was using it as a coping mechanism for his PTSD stemming from the helicopter crash. His anger was another barrier to his healing, so he needed to confess that problem too.

Reducing the noise. John embarked on a two-month hike across Colorado, and in so doing connected intimately with God. Away from civilization, he was able to avoid social media, stay away from provocative images, and shield his eyes from temptation. He had no access to electronics; it was just him and the Lord. The journey turned out to be a tremendous time of healing because John spent it praying constantly and discovered a deeper connection with the Holy Spirit than he'd experienced before. He then became able to forgive others who had wronged him and receive forgiveness himself.

Committing to studying God's Word. John knew that he had to follow God's path for his life. One verse that provided encouragement and helped him remain grounded was Philippians 4:8: "Finally, brothers [and sisters], whatever is true, whatever is honorable, whatever is just, whatever is pure, whatever is lovely, whatever is commendable, if there is any excellence, if there is anything worthy of praise, think about these things."

Dedicating himself to a life of forgiveness and reconciliation. Pornography wasn't John's only problem; his anger made things worse. But the more he gave and received forgiveness, the more evidence he saw of God's Spirit working in his life and his relationships. He found a new favorite Bible story in Luke 7:36-50, where a sinful woman anoints Jesus' feet and Jesus responds by forgiving her sins. Today, John has found that his story has turned out much the same way: *He who has been forgiven much loves much.* He used to live a life of anger, unforgiveness, and lust, but he dedicated himself to finding healing from his trauma through the power of giving and receiving forgiveness, seeking God's Spirit, and obeying His Word.

• • •

Back in Colorado, I returned to the same physical therapist I'd seen for a prior whiplash injury. I told him about some exercises that the hospital staff had suggested, and I was concerned when he started working on my hip muscles. Why wasn't he working on my neck? I noticed then that his breath smelled of alcohol and he was behaving in a forceful and aggressive manner.

I froze.

It was as if I couldn't move or even talk. I had an immediate flashback to my ex-boyfriend. I had no idea why I was thinking about him at that moment, and I tried to dismiss the flashback. I was confused by my thoughts at the time, but I now have a much better understanding. The physical therapist ended up sexually assaulting me in his office.

That was the last time I ever saw him. I reported his behavior to Colorado's regulatory department and learned that there'd been a previous complaint filed against him.

For my vision therapy, I found a great therapist, someone who was highly recommended and had a lot of experience with TBIs. Unfortunately, I had barely started the treatments when I found that each session invariably triggered another migraine. I completed three sessions in hopes that things would improve, but they didn't. The therapist was at a loss. So much for six months of treatments. So much for being able to read again.

Once again, I'd hit another roadblock, and once again there was no next step in place. After my experience with the physical therapist, I'd reached a point where I had a hard time trusting any providers, much less other people who said they could help me. My frustration with the healthcare system continued to escalate, and I had no other avenues to pursue except to trust in God's unfailing love and plan for my life. So . . . more waiting.

That summer, the Air Force decided to retire me. My reading impediment, continued migraines, and inability to serve at 100-percent capacity left them with little choice. Serving as an Air Force officer and psychiatrist had been my dream. Instead, I'd suffered another sexual assault, and I was still no closer to recovery.

REFLECTION

1. What is a major societal barrier you are facing?
2. How has modern technology (phones, social media, etc.) adversely affected your relationships?
3. What are some steps you can take in order to reduce the noise in your life?

CHALLENGE

Once you've identified a strategy to reduce the time-stealing influence of technology and other distractions on your life, ask God to help you fill the time it opens up with something life-giving and of eternal value.

CHAPTER SEVEN

overcoming physical barriers to healing

I first met Rachel when some of her friends brought her to a Tribe group meeting. She had a history of homelessness and addiction to methamphetamines and other hard drugs, but she had come to receive Christ and had been clean for several months by the time of this meeting.

After hearing me recount my journey with trauma, Rachel felt empowered to share her own experiences with childhood abuse and drug use. The more I learned about her family history, the more I realized that she needed to deal with not only her present but also her past. She suffered from dissociative episodes, flashbacks, and anger. She couldn't remember a time when members of her family weren't using drugs. In fact, she remembered them mocking her weakness when she didn't want to try certain things.

As soon as she was old enough, she joined the military in an attempt to break the cycle of sexual and substance abuse. Unfortunately, it didn't turn out to be a safe haven from the chaos and trauma of her youth. She endured a serious sexual assault in the military, and she continued to rely on marijuana to deal with the fallout from her childhood trauma. Marijuana remained her main source of comfort, as it had throughout her life, and after her military discharge, she reverted back to harder drugs in order to cope.

By the time we met, she had stopped using more dangerous substances, like methamphetamines, but her marijuana addiction was a much harder habit to break. She recognized the grip it had on her, but it seemed like the only thing that could calm her anxiety. She had grown dependent to the point that a lack of marijuana in her system caused her anxiety to worsen to the point that she could barely concentrate. Meanwhile, her addiction grew stronger. She needed ever-increasing amounts just to maintain her level of functioning.

Marijuana had been her lifelong comfort mechanism, albeit one that had perpetuated her feelings of avoidance. It had also prevented her from processing her trauma and dealing with her emotions in healthy ways. In her case, marijuana was a *physical barrier* to her healing, and it impacted every part of her life. Unless she was freed from it, she would never experience what life looked like unshackled from debilitating dependence.

We lost touch for a time after the Tribe sessions concluded, but I reconnected with her during a Veterans Day event at a local church. When I walked into the building, she ran up to me beaming. She said that the Tribe program had changed her life and helped her make tremendous progress in her healing and that she had been baptized soon after the group meetings had ended. As we talked, however, I got the impression that some of her PTSD symptoms continued to linger. She reported that she'd been zoning out a lot, even while singing at church.

This was a sign of the dissociative episodes that had long been her primary coping mechanism for avoiding trauma. Her drug use had been another means of escape, but now that she was off the hard drugs, her body increasingly relied on checking out from the current situation. She had gotten to a point where just about any threat of trauma, no matter how minor, would trigger these dissociative episodes. In those moments, she lost the ability to engage or even loosely focus on what she was doing. When I offered to set up some appointments for individual therapy, she enthusiastically agreed.

A significant aspect of her treatment was convincing her that I was her ally. She needed to be able to trust me, open up to me, and sense that I understood what she was going through. Establishing this sort of relationship takes time and a safe environment free of judgment and shame. She also needed to know that she was valued. After a lifetime of feeling dismissed, she needed someone in her life to listen to and truly hear her. She needed me to show her something different.

The good news is that she wanted to get better, to heal.

She wanted to let go of old habits and behaviors, and she was willing to put in the work. This meant that first she needed to stop running from her pain and PTSD symptoms, because continually avoiding her trauma was a continuing factor in her inability to heal from it. Second, she needed to break free from her dependence on marijuana, because in addition to decreasing her motivation and increasing her anxiety, it was preventing her from moving forward.

Throughout this process, she was also deepening her faith. She knew that God's love for her was greater than any trauma she'd ever faced, and the closer she drew to Him, the more strength she had to let go of the survival mechanisms she'd relied on for a lifetime. His love gave her the strength she needed to face the lingering pain of trauma and abandonment, because she finally knew for certain that she was accepted and cherished.

The more she recognized her identity in Christ, the less power past insults and betrayals held over her. She knew the journey wouldn't be easy, but she pressed ahead with God by her side. She tackled the less intense memories first, and her small victories gave her the sense of empowerment she needed to take on the more prominent trauma from her past. She learned to forgive those who had wronged her and discovered healthy ways to cope. She joined groups for veterans just like her and found the strength to share her story in a safe setting. In so doing, she even empowered the people around her.

But, as if her issues weren't already difficult enough, she also dealt with attention deficit hyperactivity disorder (ADHD).

She'd struggled with it throughout her childhood and in the military, but the VA wouldn't prescribe her ADHD medication due to her history of substance abuse, particularly with methamphetamines. This turned out to be the final motivation that she needed to get off all drugs for good.

So what led to her success? She finally confronted the dissociation—those feelings of being detached from her environment, the people around her, and even her own body—that she had struggled with for much of her life. Drugs, particularly marijuana, were a major part of this maladaptive defense mechanism. In her case, dissociation was a coping method that helped her escape both the trauma of her childhood and the subsequent traumas that had followed. Some of these life events had been so overwhelming that she'd used any means possible to check out.

Not only were drugs a simple way to avoid the pain, but they also made it easier for her to dissociate. Thus, the more she was able to break the grip of harder drugs, the more she realized just how much she still relied on marijuana to cope with her PTSD. (It didn't help that recreational marijuana is legal in Colorado.) After first working through her earlier traumas and then her military trauma, she reached a point where she was no longer dealing with dissociation throughout the day. But even as she gained more confidence in the healing process, marijuana remained her way to check out. When she at last saw marijuana for what it was—a means of avoidance that also perpetuated her PTSD symptoms—she was finally convinced to stop using it once and for all.

She wanted to make sure her addictions were really behind her, so she entered a rehabilitation center to gain the necessary coping skills she'd need. It certainly wasn't easy, but after a month of sobriety from marijuana, she started to experience more clarity and less anxiety. And as she began taking medication for her ADHD, she regained more of her focus and ability to concentrate.

Her resolve to finally remove marijuana as a barrier began with her recognition that it was a problem. She participated in a rehab program that emphasized accountability and support. She made better decisions regarding her daily activities and worked to maintain an environment of peace and safety. She learned to lean on her faith to help overcome the darkness that had plagued her throughout her life. Finally, recognizing that her ADHD symptoms were a barrier that kept her from returning to school and finding a new career gave her newfound motivation to treat them.

Rachel found healing from her trauma by . . .

Recognizing that her marijuana use was adversely affecting her overall health.

Committing to getting professional treatment for her mental health through individual and group therapy, rehabilitation, and carefully monitored medication instead of only self-medication.

Identifying the lies and misconceptions she believed about her sense of value and self-worth.

Finding her comfort and identity in God instead of in her lifelong coping mechanism of substance abuse.

Seeking empowerment by healing from her past traumas in order to better navigate current and future challenges.

●　●　●

Physical barriers to healing not only prevent personal and physical recovery but can also contribute to isolation, avoidance, and the inability to control or regulate one's emotional responses. (I've heard trauma sufferers say that they don't want to take chemicals that could alter their brain chemistry but continue to use marijuana and alcohol.) While drug and alcohol abuse are some of the most common physical barriers to healing, so is using any substance as a substitute for addressing underlying issues. Prescription medications can be one example of this. Medications are game changers for some people, but they can also be abused.

When properly administered, prescription sedatives can be helpful. And yet, just like marijuana and alcohol, they often numb emotions and create what seems like a quick fix to trauma. These substances can make someone feel better for the moment, but the change is only temporary and usually makes things worse. Marijuana, one of the most common substances, can contribute to paranoia, rebound anxiety, decrease motivation, and, when used in adolescence, reduce IQ. Alcohol and sedatives, meanwhile, can inhibit deep sleep cycles, which in turn inhibits memory processing, recovery, and the feeling of restfulness that we all need. As we saw in Rachel's case, excessive use of addictive substances often leads to increased tolerance and dependence.

When dealing with trauma, psychological pain can often be manifested as physical pain, and physical pain invariably takes a toll on one's mental state. Unresolved anger can lead to physical issues, like cardiovascular disease, insulin resistance, hypertension, and chronic pain. Women who have experienced sexual assault also report more problems with chronic pain than women who haven't. When addressing physical barriers, it is vital to see how the entire person—mind and body—is affected and what exactly is perpetuating the suffering.

In my experience as a psychiatrist, many people who have no problem seeking help for physical ailments are nonetheless reluctant to seek help for mental or emotional issues—and only then as a last resort. But it is critical for those struggling with anxiety, trauma, and depression to be evaluated by both a physician and a mental-health professional in order to move forward. Physical problems do not occur in a vacuum. Without a conclusive diagnosis, it is unwise to separate issues of the body from issues of the mind.

Other physical barriers to healing include improper diet, poor self-care, and even refusal to acknowledge the reality of a situation. In order to get better, a trauma patient typically needs to acknowledge that treatment is necessary. For a long time after my traumatic brain injury, I remained in denial about the limitations it imposed on my physical health. Over and over I tried to push through my headaches, ignore my body's groanings, and do the same things I could do before the event. This negative cycle led to more setbacks, more migraines, and more misery.

• • •

Have you ever desired something so much that you lost sight of everything else around you? This was my primary mode of operation for much of my life. I was a goal-oriented, achievement-focused individual who always accomplished what I set out to accomplish. I thought this was a great character trait . . . until it wasn't. Laid low by my traumatic brain injury, I could no longer simply put on blinders and proceed full steam ahead.

Forget about goals and achievements—I was now incapable of doing much of anything. I was isolated and unable to work. I couldn't read without it triggering intense migraines and nausea. But my goal never changed: I was committed to getting better so that I could go back to work as a psychiatrist and Air Force officer. I wanted to help others again. God, however, knew that I needed healing first—not just in my body, but also in my soul.

I visited neurologists, psychologists, psychiatrists, chiro-practors, physical therapists, vestibular therapists, occupa-tional therapists, speech therapists—basically every sort of specialist you can think of. I tried many medications and numerous treatment centers. Each time I was hopeful, but nothing seemed to work. It felt like I was trapped in the movie *Groundhog Day*, longing to be well, but never getting there.

In 2018, as I embarked on yet another specialized pro-gram, I was optimistic that this would be the one to finally give me healing. It was designed for veterans, and I'd learned about it from a new friend I'd made during my first TBI treatment in Texas. The program lasted over two months, cost more than $30,000, and took me about a year to get into. I spent the first month in Dallas, working with TBI specialists, neurologists, and other professionals. The next month I spent in Virginia, where I addressed the physical aspects of my TBI, like rebuilding my strength. At this point, I'd been out of the Air Force for about six months, and I was, as always, hoping to get my life back.

After two months of specialized treatment, I enjoyed some minor improvements, but my migraines were still a daily occurrence, and I still couldn't read. I wasn't healed—not even close. I was feeling very down, and I remember sitting in a church service along with hundreds of strangers. The pastor looked in my direction. "Some of you here are angry at God," he said. "It's because you are placing something above God that He has not given you."

It was like the pastor was speaking to me. God had not given me the healing that I so desperately wanted. I was sure He was withholding good from me. I felt like Eve in the Garden of Eden after the serpent deceived her: *Why can't I eat the fruit from that tree? Why won't God let me have what I want?*

In that moment, I recognized that I had placed my desire for healing above my desire for God. Without realizing it, I had once again donned my blinders; I could see nothing beyond my desperate search for a cure. The pastor was right—I was angry. I believed that God had put me on a shelf. Why hadn't He made me a productive member of society again? I knew that I needed to repent and shift my perspective.

• • •

How often do we blame God for our misfortunes and for not giving us what we think we need? In that moment, He began to teach me that He always gives me what I need, though not necessarily what I want. He also showed me that He can use my trauma for good in some way. As I reflected on my misery, I began to see the wisdom of Job when he said, "The Lord gave, and the Lord has taken away; blessed be the name of the Lord" (Job 1:21) and "Though he slay me, I will hope in him" (Job 13:15). On a flight back to Colorado, God whispered His love and hope into my soul. Because I still couldn't write without migraines, I dictated the following prayer into my phone:

My desire is to dwell in His presence forever, to never stop seeking His face, and to seek Him rightly as He is. I'm tired of the lies the enemy keeps whispering to try to disqualify me from the race. I pray that the thick fog from this brain injury will lift. I pray that God will open the eyes of my heart so that I can see with spiritual eyes the purpose, power, and authority that I have in this life, despite the feebleness I feel. This life is a battle, a war fought alongside our King. Although we are assailed on every side, we will be victorious. Christ has conquered death and sin; all that's left is to help rescue as many captives as we can.

"I believe that I shall look upon the goodness of the Lord in the land of the living! Wait for the Lord; be strong, and let your heart take courage; wait for the Lord!" (Psalm 27:13-14).

Where do you turn when every move you make toward progress and hope leads to disappointment and frustration? Where do you turn when the darkness won't relent and it takes all your strength to hold on to the glimmer of light? Where do you turn when you try to stay focused on what is right, good, and true but cannot seem to lift yourself out of the pit? It had been almost three years, and there was no end in sight. I was tired of not being the helper and instead being the helpless and needy one stuck in a pit of despair.

The only place I knew to turn was to the face of Jesus Christ. It was time to look to the hills and remember where my help comes from: the maker of heaven and earth. I was going back to the high country to kindle a reawakening in my soul that no amount of pain, disappointment, or nausea could snuff out.

• • •

Sleep (or rather, lack thereof) was another physical barrier to my healing. Prior to my TBI, I had little trouble falling or staying asleep. I rarely even thought about it. Post-injury, however, my sleep routine was significantly disrupted, and I experienced insomnia and intense restlessness almost every night.

I eventually discovered a medication that helped me fall asleep within about thirty minutes. This medication was what's known as a sedative hypnotic: It helps people fall asleep, but this isn't a restful or restorative sleep—much like the way excessive alcohol makes people tired but doesn't lead to quality rest. And not getting the deep sleep you need creates a hormone depletion that can inhibit memory and physical recovery. I eventually reached a point where I was not able to fall asleep without this medication. The more I took it, the more dependent on it I became. Soon I was afraid not to take it, because if I didn't get enough sleep, I was more prone to migraines. It was a vicious cycle, and I needed to break it.

Up to this point, I had not been very intentional about my sleep habits. I'd simply relied on the medication. I decided that it was time to establish a routine. I started abiding by the two-hour rule: No large meals, intense exercise, television, electronics, or stressful conversations or situations for at least two hours before bed, and definitely no phones, computers, or other screens in bed. Keeping my bedroom at a cool temperature, below 68°F, was also helpful, as was taking a hot bath or shower before bed. Perhaps most important of all was sticking to a routine. I was intentional about going to sleep around the same time each night whenever possible and getting up at about the same time each morning. I started taking some natural supplements to help me relax, and I incorporated mindfulness, breathing exercises, and journaling to help combat my body's hypervigilant state (largely due to my past trauma). This way, I was able to target both mental and physical restlessness. After about a month on my new routine, I was able to wean off the sleeping medication.

"Rest in Christ" became a recurring theme in my life and recovery. I needed to stop striving and let God fight my battles. Moreover, I needed to trust that He was fighting for me. He is my strength in times of weakness. He wants the best for me. I had to start trusting in Him and leaning not on my own understanding. He is the way of life. No matter what I experienced in my body and mind, I resolved to pursue the Lord with all I had. And as I pursued Him, I began the process of getting out of my own way.

• • •

In my monthlong treatment program in Texas, I was diagnosed with PTSD stemming from the initial sexual assault from my ex-boyfriend. I was still in denial about it, and I was working so hard to defend myself, protect myself, and avoid future pain that it took a tremendous toll on me. I needed to get out of isolation. I needed to confide in someone with fresh ears. I needed a professional who could help me address my issues from a spiritual as well as a psychological perspective. I found a therapist who shared my faith, and it led to the breakthrough I needed.

I received physical healing from my trauma by . . .

Seeking out professionals who could help identify the source of my physical issues—well-rounded specialists who endeavored to treat both mind and body.

Becoming honest and transparent with myself and others and being willing to accept that mental and spiritual components both contributed to my physical symptoms.

Developing a habit of self-reflection instead of dismissing my past and living in denial.

Incorporating better self-care, healthy eating, distress management skills, and an ongoing routine for better sleep.

Acknowledging the deep roots of my anger, bitterness, and resentment that stemmed from my trauma and allowing God to absorb and heal the wounds in my soul.

REFLECTION

1. What is a major physical barrier in your life? What can you do to address it?
2. What physical vices do you gravitate toward? When did you start relying on these coping mechanisms?
3. At what times or in what situations are those vices harder to avoid?

CHALLENGE

Identify a specific physical barrier and develop a strategy to help eliminate temptation as much as possible. This can include implementing accountability with others, limiting your accessibility, and identifying any underlying issues you are trying to cover up. Don't avoid seeking professional help if necessary.

trauma and suicide

When the effects of trauma are severe—or when a sufferer exhibits signs of isolation, helplessness, and despair—the possibility of suicide is often a concern. Suicide is obviously a barrier to healing, but it doesn't fit into a single category. Depression, mood disorders, addictions, and anxiety can all contribute to suicidal thoughts and behaviors.

Suicidal individuals typically experience a sense of hopelessness and worthlessness. They feel that there is no way out. From a spiritual standpoint, this is the enemy's ultimate lie—that a person's life no longer has value. And the fallout from suicide is rarely limited to a single individual; countless others are left behind to pick up the emotional pieces.

There is a crisis of suicide around the world and in the United States. According to the World Health Organization, over 700,000 people die by suicide each year.[1] In the United States, between 45,000 and 50,000 people commit suicide each year, with more than one million attempts annually.[2] Some of the most at-risk populations for suicide are military veterans and emergency responders. For example, about eighteen veterans on average end their lives each day in the United States.[3]

As a psychiatrist, I perform a safety assessment and evaluate the suicide risk of every patient I see. Of course, it's impossible to predict every suicidal act, but there are certain factors to look for. The most effective way to reduce suicides is to reduce or eliminate the risk factors. These risk factors include the following:

* feelings of isolation
* lack of community support
* a history of suicide attempts
* relational stressors, such as infidelity, failed relationships, the loss or suicide of a loved one, bullying, or sexual assault
* a feeling that God is distant and punitive
* financial distress
* chronic physical or mental illness
* a history of trauma
* physical, emotional, or sexual abuse

* drug or alcohol abuse
* limited access to physical/mental health services

If you or someone you know is struggling with suicidal thoughts or behaviors, it's vital to seek professional help as soon as possible. A mental-health professional can perform a safety assessment and identify barriers that need to be addressed, as well as how to best support the individual moving forward. Hidden intentions of the heart are powerful, but once revealed, they lose much of their power. This is why therapy and counseling can be very effective.

I've worked with many people who have been in such a state of depletion. The prophet Isaiah uses the poetic language of "bruised reeds" and "faintly burning wicks" to refer to these individuals who are in a state of depletion, struggling spiritually, physically, or morally, yet who can still find healing and restoration. How does God respond to these damaged people? Should they be left behind or discarded? Of course not. He will restore them: "A bruised reed he will not break, and a faintly burning wick he will not quench; he will faithfully bring forth justice" (Isaiah 42:3).

Through my work with veterans and first responders, I believe that God has used me as a vessel to help heal bruised reeds and smoldering wicks—people who feel trapped or like they have no way out or who are hurting deeply, their flames growing fainter. When I met the following two patients, they were on the brink of total hopelessness. I suspected they were on the verge of suicide. But God allowed me to help bridge that gap between life and death. I was able to show up for them, to fan their flames, and to point them toward life.

• • •

I first shared Scott's story in chapter 4, when we looked at spiritual barriers to healing from trauma. He became part of our Advancing Warriors community through one of my Tribe groups for veterans. Soon he was volunteering his time and serving in the community, but he still occasionally struggled with depression and thoughts of suicide.

As he learned to trust others, he started reaching out to members of his Tribe group. He also reached out to me, especially when he was struggling with suicidal thoughts. He called me when he felt like he was at the end of himself, and we would talk and pray while I tried to help him redirect his thoughts. Many of these times, he would have rather been alone, but he called anyway. Deep down, he knew that he needed a lifeline.

He continued to struggle until that life-changing night when his fellow warriors gathered around him to pray for him. He knew without a doubt that the other group members cared about him, that I cared about him, and—most important of all—that God cared about him. And it was this recognition that caused his suicidal thoughts to dissipate. His struggle with suicidal thoughts subsided through a relentless pursuit of what God wanted for him, reinforced by friends and his wife helping him climb out of the place where he was drowning.

Scott overcame his suicidal thoughts and behaviors by . . .

Letting others in. This is probably the most important step in preventing suicide. One reason many people who have lost loved ones this way didn't recognize the warning signs is that the hurting individual never acknowledged their pain. Scott, however, opened up about his hurt to his Tribe group and to me. And when he finally exposed his vulnerability, he experienced not rejection but unconditional love.

Seeking professional help. There are numerous mental-health providers, hotlines, and crisis centers available to help anyone who is struggling with suicidal thoughts. Scott was willing to reach out to me for help, especially in those moments when his well-being was in danger. Anytime someone displays even a hint of suicidal behavior, seeking professional help is critical.

Recognizing the risk factors. I worked with Scott to help him identify the factors that contributed to his suicidality, including alcohol use and isolation. He then agreed to be accountable for his actions in order to avoid those triggers. Substance abuse, for example, can cause depression, disinhibition, and reduced reasoning, as well as perpetuate the urge to self-harm. Exploring his past trauma enabled Scott to recognize his risk factors and the ongoing patterns of behavior that led him to crash and burn after striving to prove himself. He needed to unlearn his self-destructive coping mechanisms and instead lean on God for affirmation.

Committing to healing. Scott agreed to maintain sobriety from alcohol and committed to praying, reading the Bible, and being honest with others about the struggles in his life.

• • •

Jessica showed up at my office one night and informed me that I was her last resort. She had already tried multiple medications, individual therapy, and counseling, all without success. She told me she'd lived her entire life without a sense of belonging, without feeling heard, without feeling loved. She was hopeless and depressed, convinced that her relationships were all beyond repair.

During my initial evaluation, she said that she felt like a burden to everyone in her life, including her husband and children. She didn't know where else to turn and said that if I couldn't help her right away, she intended to end her life. She refused to check into a hospital, so my best—my only—strategy was to buy more time. Putting a seventy-two-hour psychiatric hold on her could jeopardize her trust in me, so thankfully, I convinced her to give me at least two weeks.

Jessica needed hope. She needed purpose. She needed to discover her true identity. She kept asking for help but felt ignored. She had made her first suicide attempt when she was a teenager, but everyone in her life had seemed to dismiss it. The emergency room staff had even suggested that she was simply seeking attention. When I asked her about her faith, she said that she believed in God but that He had not been there for her in the past.

Was she willing to explore her faith some more?

"I'll do whatever it takes," she said.

She was not attending church at the time, but she said that she was open to it. She had a lot of anxiety around crowds, however, and would not go alone, so I offered to meet her there. I also suggested some medication to help her feel better and convinced her that we should continue working together. She agreed.

When we met at church, I could sense her anxiety and walked her through some breathing exercises to help her relax. We sat in the back of the room so we could slip out easily if necessary. Even with all my preparations, I still wasn't prepared for her reaction. She began to weep during the very first worship song and continued to cry throughout the service. I did my best to comfort her.

The sermon that day included a video about a man from the church who'd lost a brother to suicide, recounting the impact it had had on his life. After the message was over, we walked out early, and Jessica turned to me.

"You knew what they were going to talk about, didn't you?" she asked.

I assured her that I'd had no idea what the sermon would be about, much less the video, especially since the church didn't share those topics in advance. She didn't believe me until she asked the church staff for herself. In fact, they told her, that particular video clip had originally been scheduled for the previous weekend but had been postponed a week due to a technical malfunction.

I didn't know it at the time, but Jessica told me later that she had planned to end her life that very night. Instead, that church service was part of a special encounter she had with the Lord. For the first time in her life, she felt like God was pursuing her. She felt valued. She felt hope. Instead of ending her life, she decided to keep pressing forward.

This was not the last time that she had suicidal thoughts or seriously contemplated an attempt. The isolation stemming from her past trauma, failed relationships, depression, and anxiety remained a significant barrier. Still, a seed was planted that night. The idea that God cared about her as an individual was a foreign concept to her, and she began to ponder it in her heart.

We made it through those first two weeks, and the weeks turned into months. About a year after her initial breakthrough, however, she found herself at rock bottom once more. She turned to alcohol as her coping mechanism, which caused emotional dysregulation, impulsivity, and depression. She tried to fire her therapist, marriage counselor, and me on multiple occasions. She began cutting herself and fantasizing about death. But no matter what she did, her mental-health team never gave up on her.

As a child, she had asked for help but had felt ignored. As an adult, when her husband found her with a loaded gun, everyone took her very seriously. Her husband called the police, and she was admitted to the hospital. She could no longer claim that no one cared or that she was being dismissed.

It was a major turning point in her life. She had to decide whether to surrender or to fight. She decided to fight. She decided to live. She began by giving up alcohol and ridding her life of toxic relationships. She realized that she wanted to stick around for those who loved her. She started taking medication to give her emotional stability, and she began to really trust her therapists and me, recognizing that we never stopped supporting her even at her lowest moment. Most importantly, she committed her life to following Jesus Christ.

She took up paddleboarding as a form of exercise and self-care, and she found a group of new friends as a result. With previous relationships, she had felt like people had always wanted something from her and always expected her best behavior. Growing up, for example, she'd felt like her mother had tended to favor her sister. While she craved her mother's unconditional love, she had never met her mother's expectations. Try as she might, she'd never fit the right mold.

Her new friends were a different story. After opening up to one friend about her history of suicidal thoughts, she got an unexpected response. "I don't care if you are depressed, look like a mess, or are exhausted," the friend said. "I just want you to show up." This was a foreign concept for her. Her new friend's "just show up" attitude helped reinforce the concept of God's unconditional love. The friend didn't expect anything from her; she just wanted her to be herself.

As she learned to create healthy boundaries in her relationships, she gained more confidence as God's beloved daughter. As others accepted her unconditionally, she discovered how to accept herself.

Jessica overcame her suicidal thoughts and behaviors by . . .

Acknowledging the truth after she hit rock bottom. It took a brush with death for Jessica to grasp the finality of suicide and the pain it would cause to everyone around her. As a wife, mother, daughter, sister, and friend, she finally recognized the implications of her actions.

Feeling heard. Jessica needed to know that she was taken seriously. She'd spent much of her life feeling like she didn't matter, eventually reaching the false conclusion that no one would really miss her if she was gone. When she ended up in the hospital, she finally recognized her misguided thinking.

Discovering her worth. Jessica had spent years trying to earn the approval of others. She'd made choices based not on what she wanted but on what she thought other people wanted her to do. This behavior was exhausting, confusing, and ultimately impossible. Once she recognized her value as a child of God, she was able to give up this fruitless pursuit.

Committing to self-care. Jessica let go of many barriers in her life, including toxic friendships, alcohol, and self-destructive patterns of behavior. In their place, she implemented positive coping skills, such as mindfulness and regular exercise (in the form of paddleboarding), established regular routines, and fostered healthy friendships. She discovered how to self-regulate instead of relying on substances or unhealthy behaviors.

Learning to trust. Jessica's time in the hospital also taught her that the people closest to her would not abandon her. She filled her new social circle with people of good character who truly cared about her. She developed confidence in her new identity and was able to pour into others' lives as well.

Deciding to follow Jesus no matter what. Jessica recognized that her life was not her own and that the only way to truly thrive would be in a lifelong relationship with God. That is, after all, what she was created for.

• • •

If you're wondering about my own journey: The truth is that, yes, I did contemplate suicide. Actually, I did more than just think about it.

More than a year after my fall on Longs Peak, I was in a very dark place. I had suffered a sexual assault, which I'd then tried to bury. I'd been forced to give up my career as an Air Force officer, and I was still unable to read. I felt trapped and distant from God.

The shadows surrounded me, and in a weak moment, I gave in. I was riding in a friend's car when I tried to push open my door and jump out into traffic. My friend immediately reached over to stop me.

A few minutes later we sat parked on the side of the road. The whole thing felt like an out-of-body experience—like I hadn't not been actually thinking about my actions, only acting. It was a self-destructive behavior, a maladaptive coping mechanism, an impulsive means of escape. There hadn't been a plan. Rather, in the heat of the moment, instead of facing my issues and going to God in prayer or seeking the wise counsel of a friend, I'd just sought my own way out. I thank God every day that someone was able to stop me. But I know what it feels like to have an overwhelming urge to escape the pain of living.

One of the important things I learned from this experience is that most emotional suffering is temporary. Often we simply need to wait on God for the relief we crave. Of course, this won't necessarily stop us from trying to resolve our issues on our own, though doing so often leads to dead ends. Through my own roller-coaster ride to recovery, which was filled with countless setbacks, I learned that I could endure suffering longer than I thought.

After sustaining a traumatic brain injury and developing PTSD, I also displayed an impulsivity I'd never had before. I lost my stoic filter on my emotions and interactions with others. This was both bad and good. At first I was more irritable and disrespectful to others. I went through a dark and intense depression that I just couldn't shake—desperation followed by numbness. Nothing mattered to me anymore. I was torn between the urge to abandon this life and an elusive glimmer of hope that beckoned me to stay. And yet . . . I eventually learned how to deal with this flood of emotions. With the assistance of a therapist, I began allowing myself to feel and express emotions that I had suppressed in the past.

Many people speak about the selfishness of suicide. I never really thought or worried about how my death might affect others. I never considered the idea that I had no right to take my own life. Somewhere deep down I knew that my life was not my own, but those verses were forgotten in the moment, overpowered by the desire to escape my suffering. I didn't want to die, but I definitely wanted the pain to stop. I can only imagine that it was God who held me together in those moments.

I never understood it before—how someone could end their life. But now I do. The despair that I felt then? Today it helps me empathize with others in a similar emotional state. I know from experience how to minimize my heartache and downplay the extent of my anguish. That's why it's imperative that we pay attention when a loved one is struggling.

That's sometimes easier said than done. Trauma is a powerful taskmaster. It tempts us to isolate ourselves, thinking we will protect others from our pain. Many people who experience suicidal thoughts feel like a burden to those around them, but this is not true. Feelings aren't reality. Circumstances aren't the full truth. While it's true that our loved ones suffer when we suffer, they can't (or shouldn't) blame themselves for our pain.

A big reason I ended up in such a dark place was my stubbornness. I refused for a long time to even acknowledge my issues with trauma, not to mention the severity of my problems. It wasn't until I finally opened up to my neurologist that things started to change. My health was suffering in several areas—physical, emotional, relational, and spiritual—so I tried to address as many of them as possible.

My neurologist put me on medication for impulsivity and mood swings that helped me feel grounded. I started eating better and tried to get more rest. I connected with loved ones, recognized the stressors in my life, and sought wise counsel. I began seeing a therapist and found a supportive community at church. Finally, I learned to give up my stubbornness and pride in favor of humility. After too many failed attempts to fix myself in my own power, I learned to lean on God's strength instead.

• • •

Trauma is not one-size-fits-all. It affects everyone differently. Thus, everyone's path to recovery is different. The process begins with identifying barriers to healing and then working with the tools at our disposal. These include individual therapy, support groups, medication, and faith-based counsel. We look to healthcare professionals, to our loved ones, and to God.

But what do you do when nothing seems to work, when the darkness presses in on every side and all you want to do is end the misery? I've seen many people in my practice who have tried multiple treatments without relief. I've seen many people who, in their own words, have tried everything but still see no way out. What do I say to them? *I've been there, my friend, and I will work with you for as long as it takes.*

No matter how hard life gets or how trapped you feel, suicide is never the answer. It's never even an option—certainly not if you care about the people in your life. Suicide creates lasting, devastating effects for those left behind. Those who love us are the ones who must pick up the pieces, sometimes for generations to come.

As a psychiatrist, I often feel like a "last responder"—the final line of defense when someone is ready to throw in the towel. I don't crave this role, but I accept it. When I sat in my own dungeon of despair for nearly three years, I tried countless times to escape on my own, but only God could set me free. In doing so, He gave me the experience—the keys—to help free others. I now feel like it's my duty to reenter that prison and unlock the chains of those who are shackled.

I overcame my suicidal thoughts and behaviors by . . .

Grasping the severity of my condition. A common barrier that prevents someone from seeking help is the notion that they don't really need it. *I'm not that bad,* they think. *I haven't gotten to that point yet. Other people need help much more than me.* That was my attitude for a long time, but I was only kidding myself. I was in denial. Unless and until trauma sufferers recognize that the alternative to receiving help is more anguish, many of them will never reach out.

Getting real with my providers. Once I was honest with myself, I could finally be honest with my healthcare providers. Sharing the truth about my issues began with my neurologist and spread to my therapist. The more I shared the whole truth with my providers, the more they were able to help me.

Escaping toxic relationships. Unhealthy relationships perpetuate chaos and destructive patterns in people's lives. They can reinforce lies about identity, trust, and acceptance that have existed for a long time—potentially since childhood. In order to find healing, people cannot remain in a chaotic environment where they are constantly triggered.

Embracing medication as necessary. Some people vehemently oppose medication, as if taking a prescription suggests mental weakness or a lack of faith. But starting a medication regimen to help improve my emotional stability was one of the best steps I ever took. Medication is often crucial, especially when dealing with severe depression and/or the risk of suicide. (Of course, it's important to consult with a doctor before taking any medication for depression. The same applies to treating mood or anxiety disorders. In short: Always check with a medical professional.)

Leaning on God. Scripture tells us that the Lord is our best source of comfort, even as we gravitate to whatever source we think might provide some relief. For example, 2 Corinthians 1:3-4 assures us that God is "the Father of mercies and God of all comfort, who comforts us in all our affliction, so that we may be able to comfort those who are in any affliction, with the comfort with which we ourselves are comforted by God." Jesus tells His disciples in John 14:27, "Peace I leave with you; my peace I give to you. . . . Let not your hearts be troubled, neither let them be afraid." And the psalmist proclaims, "Let your steadfast love comfort me according to your promise to your servant" (Psalm 119:76). While other coping methods might alleviate or numb our pain for the moment, they often make matters worse in the long run, leading to even more heartache than before. The sooner we go to God for comfort, the better.

Joining a community of spiritual support. God says that the body of Christ exists, at least in part, to help build up one another. Finding a like-minded community of grace is refreshing to one's soul and sometimes altogether necessary.

• • •

Life is a gift from God. Those of us who have received Christ as Savior know that our lives are no longer our own. We were bought with the price of His blood. Jesus died so that we might have life; it is not our right to take this gift.

When I found myself in the darkest of nights, I was faced with a choice: give in to the darkness or reach out to God's light. As the psalmist wrote, "He brought them out of darkness and the shadow of death, and burst their bonds apart. Let them thank the LORD for his steadfast love, for his wondrous works to the children of man!" (Psalm 107:14-15). In His steadfast love, God rescued me from the shadow of death, and He can do the same for you.

REFLECTION

1. Is there anyone in your life who is silently suffering, who needs your friendship or support?
2. Would you consider yourself in a dark place in life today? Have you ever had thoughts of suicide now or in the past? If so, what has kept you going?
3. What is your primary coping mechanism when trials arise? Do you prefer avoiding the issues, pushing the problem down, and trying to move on? Do you seek outside comforts to numb the pain, or do you stand and face your challenges?

GET HELP

* Don't wait to seek help if you're feeling suicidal, or even if you're simply stuck in a dark place. Talk to a psychiatrist, counselor, therapist, or pastor. Look for a support group in your area. If you don't know of any, reach out to a close friend.
* If you're thinking about committing suicide immediately, call the national crisis hotline at 1-800-273-8255 (and press "1" for the veteran crisis line).

CHALLENGE

If you do not have a wellness team of at least three friends you can trust and connect with, start working on building one now. Commit to working on self-care, whether it is physical, emotional, spiritual, or relational, and get the help you need in the specific areas you need it.

Identify times in your life when you've felt vulnerable or weak or endured trials or temptations. Ask God for forgiveness if you tried to hide your vulnerabilities, tried to cover up the pain, or tried to push through on your own. Ask Him to help you go directly to Him in your times of need. In our weakness, we can find His strength. Go to Him as soon as possible to receive the comfort of all comforts.

pathways to healing: self-awareness

I was fortunate to grow up in a loving home with a supportive family to offer me guidance. I had parents who grounded me in God's Word. But even with this foundation, I still lost my way many times. The world can be cruel and filled with such temptation that it is easy to wander away from the right path. But the beauty of being a child of God is that no matter how far we stray, the way back home is never too far away. God is always waiting to guide us back to safety. We only need to recognize when we're wandering through the thorns in pursuit of empty promises.

I committed my life to Jesus Christ as soon as I was old enough to understand what that meant. I enjoyed devotions and bedtime prayers with my family. As I got older, I sat in the front rows at church and took notes during the sermons. But my journey of faith was so focused on pleasing God through service, sacrifice, and maintaining my testimony that I lost sight of the kind of real relationship He wants.

I simply couldn't understand that I was already pleasing to Him, that I was already accepted. It felt like I was walking alongside His path but teetering on the edge. I was caught up in duty and obligation. Instead of following Him freely, I was busy following rules. This led to a major disconnect between my head and my heart.

Achieving my goals "for God" occupied the majority of my attention. Whenever I failed, I simply buried the shame and pressed on. It was as if I carried a backpack that I kept filling with all the cares of this world. I had everything I needed for my journey, but I was so weighed down by the burden of always trying to please God that I lost sight of His promises that He'll give us rest if we come to him, that He is gentle and lowly in heart, that His yoke is easy, and that His burden is light (see Matthew 11:28-30).

As my journey continued, I also found myself straying from His path, frequently distracted by other trails along the way.

In the next few chapters, we will explore how to find our way back to the road that leads to healing. We will explore the pathways of self-awareness, pursuing God above all else, implementing self-care, engaging in an authentic community, and holding on to hope through the ups and downs of life.

These pathways to healing point us toward the true healer—the freedom found in Christ—and away from the schemes of the evil one.

• • •

As we discussed earlier, denial and self-deception are major barriers to healing. In *The Body Keeps the Score*, psychiatrist and researcher Bessel van der Kolk examines in depth how the body stores traumatic emotions and memories. This phenomenon can be manifested in many forms, such as autoimmune conditions, chronic pain or tension, panic attacks, restlessness, or a feeling of adrenaline surging through the body. The trouble is that many, if not most, sufferers aren't aware of what's causing these conditions.[1]

This is why self-awareness is a major pathway to healing. It is imperative to uncover and then examine our traumatic memories and emotions in order to find relief. This includes being aware of traumas that can lead to unprocessed emotions and distorted beliefs. It also includes identifying ingrained moral wounds that will continue to fester if left unresolved.

Moral wounds are unseen emotional injuries that result when someone acts in a way that goes against their morals, or when such acts are done to them. One example of someone experiencing this would be a pacifist who is compelled to kill an invader in order to save innocent lives. Another would be a faithful husband or wife whose spouse engages in an affair.

Self-awareness also involves being conscious of maladaptive coping skills, being engaged in the moment, and not ignoring, denying, or zoning out to avoid the pain of past trauma.

• • •

After two months of largely unsuccessful treatment in Texas and Virginia, I remained laser focused on my physical issues and my ongoing inability to read. I largely discounted the psychological and spiritual effects of my past trauma. Not only did I discount those effects, but I also continued to deny them and did everything I could to push them out of my mind.

In the meantime, it felt like I was at war with my own body. I endured intense spasms in my hips, pelvis, neck, shoulders, and back. My muscles were tight and knotted. I tried massage therapy, but the knots always came back, often the very next day. When I visited a chiropractor to see if he could help my muscles relax, he suggested that the source of the problem likely wasn't my muscles, but rather the stress stored up in my body. He began by asking me to write down all my traumas.

My initial list included falls, concussions, and car accidents, but other traumas soon surfaced. When I confronted the reality of my sexual assaults, I became enraged. I was irritable, argumentative, and extremely restless. This trauma, I learned, had contributed to my migraines and muscle tension. My emotions were stirred up again, and I had no choice but to deal with them.

At the time, I viewed this whole process as just another failure.

• • •

I needed some repairs to my master bathroom, but I definitely couldn't repair anything myself. I couldn't even focus long enough to find a contractor, much less learn to do the work on my own. I ended up hiring someone based on my neighbors' recommendation—a contractor who made a lot of promises and asked for half the money up front. Then, after demolishing my bathroom in order to remodel it, he disappeared.

He eventually returned about a month later, worked for an hour or so, then vanished again. As this pattern continued, my internal reactions to how he worked terrified me. I wanted to punch him, scream in his face, and cry, all at the same time. But I did none of those things. I kept any outward display of emotions in check while I seethed inside.

At the time, I couldn't see the connections between my ex-boyfriend and this contractor. Now the parallels seem clear. Here was another male who had taken advantage of me, had betrayed me, had had access to my bedroom, and had wreaked havoc in my life. Looking back, it seems that this long-running incident contributed to my PTSD. I can't believe how blind I was! Instead of exploring how this situation might affect me uniquely, I blamed the contractor for all my emotions and internal responses. (This isn't to let the contractor off the hook, of course. It took another year, plus some intervention from the Better Business Bureau, before he finally completed the work on my bathroom.)

Throughout this ordeal, I was desperate to relax, to have my home to myself, but my body seemed unable to cooperate. In the past, my body would submit to my wishes, but now it rebelled.

As did my soul. I wanted to surrender my life and my will to God's, but I didn't know how. I prayed constantly, but it felt like something was physically getting in the way of my prayers. It felt like spiritual oppression.

Some friends told me about a Christian therapist who had great insights and lots of experience with this sort of situation, so I reached out to her and made an appointment. I didn't tell her anything about the sexual assaults, only that I'd been unable to read since suffering a traumatic brain injury in 2015.

Our first session included much prayer and confession. We discussed the hidden motives of my heart, a process that I found completely exhausting. I spent the rest of the day recovering from that session.

But I had hope. The next morning seemed to begin like all the others. *Will I be able to read today?* I was skeptical, as usual, but I picked up a book and began to read. No headache. No dizziness. No nausea. *Can this really be?* I kept on reading—and still no symptoms! I turned on my computer and started looking through nearly three years' worth of unread emails. Had God at last answered my prayers?

Will this last?

It did. I continued to read without headaches, and it was the beginning of a new stage in my spiritual growth. I learned how to continually rely on God's help to overcome my rebellious spirit. I learned how He could help me stand against the enemy. I learned how to surrender to Him. I had yet to uncover the lingering effects of my sexual trauma, but that would come later.

In the meantime, I had recovered my ability to read and reflect on God's Word. Paul's letter to the Ephesians tells us that when anything is exposed to God's light, not only will that thing become visible, but "Christ will shine on you" (Ephesians 5:13-14). If we remain in darkness—if we keep our secrets hidden—we block ourselves from receiving the light of Christ.

This light is the real power of self-awareness. As I brought my trauma out of the shadows, the light of Christ overwhelmed the darkness in me. And it can do the same for all of us.

• • •

Laura discovered my practice on the internet, making special note of the fact that I am a Christian. She was struggling with bipolar disorder and PTSD when she arrived at my office, telling me that it was hard to determine which of her symptoms were effects of the disorder and which were due to her trauma. She had already received treatment for her PTSD from multiple providers, but she had only found temporary relief. Now she wanted the perspective and experience of someone who shared her faith.

As she relayed her history, she explained that she had first developed bipolar disorder in her twenties, but her experience with trauma had dated back to her childhood, when she had been raped by a close family member. Her mother had known about the ongoing sexual abuse, but she'd told her that she wasn't allowed to tell anyone. So while she knew that what was happening was wrong, she was powerless to stop it.

A pattern formed. She grew up thinking she was worthless and without purpose. She thought that nothing she said or did mattered to anyone. She felt beaten down her entire life.

She recalled a time, before the abuse began, when she had held God in reverence, when she pretended that she could extend her hands toward heaven and touch Him. But her childlike innocence had faded long ago, battered into submission by years of trauma.

Her faith helped her survive those horrible years, but it couldn't undo her wounds. Unlike Rachel in chapter 7, she didn't turn to drugs or destructive behavior. But, like Rachel, she turned to dissociation. Disconnecting from her thoughts, surroundings, and the people around her had been her subconscious defense mechanism when she was younger, a way to escape the moments of terror she had experienced on a regular basis. And the more she practiced dissociation, the more she relied on it as a source of security. As a child, she had learned how to dissociate whenever she wanted. As an adult, however, she frequently dissociated without warning.

With little control over her symptoms, she experienced

what seemed like manic episodes. We discussed how her constant dissociation, once a protective mechanism in the midst of her trauma, was now stealing her life.

"I remember that when I was little, people could wave their hands in front of my face, and I'd be completely gone," she told me. "It was like my own superpower to escape everything."

I told her that dissociation can be a means of self-preservation, a way to find temporary relief during periods of trauma. But the enemy, meanwhile, can use it as a substitute source of comfort, something for people to turn to instead of their faith. Dissociation is also a form of avoidance, which only perpetuates the ongoing effects of trauma.

●　　●　　●

Laura's lightbulb moment occurred when she recognized that the way she had survived her childhood trauma had become a roadblock to her healing. Dissociation, once her most powerful means of self-comfort, was now contributing to her deterioration. Once we identified the issue, her newfound self-awareness empowered her to give up this maladaptive coping mechanism. She had a fresh pathway to healing as she learned to live more in the moment and resist the urge to dissociate.

As we prayed together, she confessed to God that she'd been using dissociation as a way to escape trauma, as a comfort instead of going to Him. She began to repent of that decision and the broad effect it had had on her life:

God, I surrender this escape and comfort over to You, and I receive You as my comfort. Help me find rest in You as my protector. Please work with me to transform my decisions so that I can stop frantically trying to fix or transform myself.

I sometimes tell patients like Laura that it's difficult to fixate on trauma—to be stuck in the past or worry about the future—when you are focused on your five senses: I say, "Focus on the present, on the current circumstances and location. Concentrate on the signs of life: inhaling and exhaling, the motion of your rib cage, the heart beating in your chest. Try to focus on who you are, what you're doing, and where you are now." Laura had been encouraged to practice some of these techniques by a previous therapist, but she hadn't really given it much consideration.

As she continued to focus on God as her comfort, she found that these little tactics helped. Her dissociative episodes began to dissipate, and she was able to regain control over her body.

Laura found a pathway to healing from trauma by . . .

Never giving up. Laura was persistent, and she continued to seek help despite multiple unsuccessful attempts over a span of decades. She tried multiple medications, experimental procedures, and therapies, never quitting until she found the best pathway to recovery for her.

Improving her self-awareness. Laura learned that her lifelong habit of dissociation was a hindrance to her healing.

Many methods of coping with stress and trauma end up becoming excessive or destructive in the end. For example, a recurring habit of comfort eating can lead to diabetes, obesity, and cardiovascular issues if left unchecked. Without self-awareness, persistent unhealthy habits or attachments can become idols of sorts, impeding our relationships with God.

Recognizing the spiritual battle. Laura was often tempted to check out of the present and revert to her old comfort zone. Her dissociation, however, prevented her from achieving her potential in Christ. It kept her from working, sharing her testimony, and interacting with hurting people who need the Lord. She realized what was going on, confessed her maladaptive habit, and turned to God as her comforter and protector.

* * *

After my tumultuous relationship with my ex-boyfriend, I felt like used goods. My sense of worth had taken a big hit, and I tried to suppress any thoughts that tarnished my reputation. In my mind, the solution was simple: I'd find someone new—someone better—to make up for my mistakes. So I returned to the dating apps and went on multiple dates. But I was still chasing my childhood fantasy of finding a man who would complete me.

Then a man I knew through a friend began pursuing me on Facebook. He told me he was a Christian. He told me he was pursuing God. He checked all the right boxes. When we were alone, however, he pushed me for physical intimacy past my point of comfort. I tried to maintain firm physical boundaries, but I let things go too far. Every time I hung out with him, I felt sick about messing up yet again.

I longed to be appreciated, to feel desired, and it took a timely sermon at church to show me just how desperately I was chasing after affirmation. The pastor described sin as a window into our hearts, and he urged us to seek God's help in identifying what was perpetuating our behavior. As I reflected on this question, God helped me see that my dating behavior—in particular, the desperate need I felt to find a partner—was the real window into my heart. There was a void in my soul that I was trying to fill with a romantic relationship instead of with God.

I had another lightbulb moment that night: I had fallen into a pattern of settling, of lowering my standards and modifying my morals in order to find someone who would appreciate me. Feeling desired, valued, and adored was my priority. Even though I enjoyed all those blessings through the Father, Son, and Holy Spirit, I continued to seek them elsewhere. The pastor's message that day helped me see how I wanted to become a woman who was desired by men instead of the woman God wanted me to be.

The enemy had a foothold, but I didn't realize what it was until the evening of that church service. I was probably afraid to confront my flaws because they would only confirm that I was a mess. Instead of allowing God to transform me, I had become plagued with self-condemnation. It finally clicked that night that sin was a window through which God's light would shine onto the lies I'd believed.

For years I'd tried covering up my sin, ignoring it in hopes that it would go away. Now I felt empowered to go to God with my mistakes, to ask for His help as I explored the source of my misguided thinking. This shift in perspective made all the difference. Just as Adam and Eve couldn't hide their sin with fig leaves, I couldn't simply cover my guilt and shame. There is only one covering for sin: the blood that Christ shed for us on the cross.

God's light is like the power of self-awareness, of knowing right from wrong. What was once the source of Adam and Eve's Fall can today serve as a pathway to healing, thanks to Christ's sacrifice and offer to illuminate the darkness within us.

The seeds of my moral wounds had been planted during childhood when I was molested, and those wounds had continued to accumulate with each subsequent trauma. Each time, I lost more and more of my innocence. Even after I asked God to heal my wounds, I still didn't achieve a breakthrough until I allowed myself to see what He sees because of Christ: a child running into the arms of her Father— embraced, accepted, and fully loved.

That's when I recognized that true holiness is only found in Christ. I was finally free from the constant thoughts of being tainted, undesirable, filthy. I had always known my value in God's eyes, but now I could visualize it for myself. I could sense it. I could feel it. The more I embraced my child-like wonder—my awe of God and what He had done for me—the more my irritability, self-hatred, impatience, and rigidity melted away.

• • •

I met Sharon while working in a hospital during my psychiatry residency. She was living with lupus and was in the medical unit due to heart complications. The admitting physician ordered a psychiatric consultation because he wondered if her depression was affecting her recovery. She had never spoken to anyone about an incident that had preceded her depression and her lupus, but she decided it was finally time to share about an experience that had caused her a lot of pain.

Her son, Jake, had just returned from overseas duty in the military. He was struggling emotionally, and she did not know how to help him. One day, he called and asked her to get his military uniform dry-cleaned and pressed. He spoke to her about his belief in God, and when he said that suicide did not prevent someone from entering heaven, she knew that something was very wrong. She called 911 from another phone and tried to keep him on the line until the police arrived. When Jake heard the police sirens in the distance, he asked, "Did you call the police?"

Then she heard a single gunshot.

That moment changed her life forever. In her head, she kept replaying the events leading up to that fatal moment. *What could I have done differently? What should I have said?* She worried about her son's soul. *Would someone who has committed suicide go to hell?*

The pain was too much. Her body collapsed under the strain, and she developed her lupus soon after. She also fell into deep depression that remained untreated. She never let herself grieve, and she never spoke to anyone about the incident.

In the medical unit, we talked about what the Bible says about suicide. We discussed the story of Samson, who ended his own life when God gave him the strength to avenge himself against the wicked Philistines (see Judges 16:23-31). I pointed out that in Hebrews 11 Samson is praised for his faith, which I think is evidence that he may be in heaven. We discussed the grace and forgiveness of God that is available to all.

"Do you think my son could be in heaven?" she asked.

I nodded and said, "If he trusted in Jesus Christ as Savior, absolutely. Salvation is not based on the works that we do or don't do but on our faith in Jesus' finished work on the cross."

As she considered this new hope, her face brightened. She looked like a different person. It was as if a tremendous burden had been lifted and she could smile again for the first time in years. We then discussed what it would take for her to get outpatient treatment for depression, invest in self-care, and allow herself to grieve the death of her son through therapy.

The thought of Jake being in hell had hindered her ability to grieve and likely contributed to her physical and mental decline. For years she had held on to that pain, blaming herself that she hadn't done enough to keep him alive. Once she understood the cause of her trauma—once she became self-aware—she was able to begin healing physically, emotionally, and spiritually. She was able to live again.

Sharon found a pathway to healing from her trauma by . . .

Identifying the cause. It's difficult to explain just how closely the mind, body, and spirit are all connected. When people develop depression, for example, it can affect their appetite, energy, and sleep. When people hold on to anger, bitterness, or resentment, it can affect their cardiovascular health, cortisol levels, and tension in their bodies. Conversely, when people pray and seek treatment for emotional pain or deep wounds of the soul, beautiful healing can occur.

Uncovering the lies. Sharon believed she could have somehow prevented Jake's suicide. It's actually a common issue with people who have lost loved ones this way: They obsess about all the potential warning signs they missed. They replay the events in their heads. They wonder, *If I'd said certain words in a certain way, would my loved one still be alive?* Sharon could continue to beat herself up about what she could or might have done, but that was pointless. Instead, she concluded that it was time to start moving forward again.

Committing to getting help. For too long, Sharon lived in the past, blaming herself for the loss of her son. She didn't want to move on without him—to the point that she couldn't. The despair she felt even prevented her from taking care of herself. In her mind, she felt like she didn't deserve to heal. That all changed when she committed to getting better. Once freed from guilt and introduced to hope, she rediscovered the spark of life she needed to enjoy life.

REFLECTION

1. Where do you turn in order to insulate yourself from emotional pain and vulnerability?
2. How might you lean on God for protection and comfort instead of trying to push through or bury your painful emotions?
3. Consider again the truth spoken in Ephesians 5:13-14: "When anything is exposed by the light, it becomes visible, for anything that becomes visible is light. Therefore it says, 'Awake, O sleeper, and arise from the dead, and Christ will shine on you.'" Are there areas in your life where you feel like you have been asleep?
4. How might you have passively accepted a lie that continues to control you?

CHALLENGE

Prayerfully read through Psalm 139. Consider how much God cares for you despite knowing all your darkest thoughts and behaviors. Let Psalm 139:23-24 be your prayer. Ask God to search your heart and illuminate anything that might be holding you back from reaching your full potential in Christ. As you pray, write down what the Holy Spirit brings to your mind.

pathways to healing:
pursuing God

Humankind was created in the image of God, yet we easily lose sight of our creator. We seek after wealth and fame, honor and prestige, respect and success—longings of this world that never fully satisfy. Things get even worse when these priorities become our masters.

The desire for worldly validation can appear noble at times. We think we have the best of intentions until we realize that we've prioritized other pursuits ahead of God. These can even be otherwise good pursuits, like ministry, health, or our families. The distinction is subtle, but it's all too common: Often we pursue peace or joy instead of the Giver of peace and joy. I fell into this trap myself when I pursued healing over the Healer.

I definitely grieved when my Air Force days ended, but it also gave me the freedom to partner with God in new and powerful ways. I felt like He was saying to me, *You have been trained in the world's wisdom. Now let me train you in My wisdom, which brings real healing to those in need.*

Three years after the accident on Longs Peak that changed my life, I was finally able to read—and work—without constant migraines. That was good news. The not-so-good news? I still struggled with chronic pain, irritability, and loneliness. And, of course, there was still that disdain for the home contractor I'd hired.

The treatments I'd engaged with were helping, but they didn't erase the anger inside me. My survival instinct, my need to escape the threats I felt on a daily basis, was out of control.

Self-awareness, apparently, can only get you so far. Being aware of my rage wasn't necessarily enough to take the rage away. I also experienced an intense restlessness, and peace evaded me. I needed a deeper cleansing of the soul that secular therapy could not provide. So I decided to return to my Christian therapist. I knew that if I started treating patients too soon, I ran the risk of reacting to their problems in irrational ways. My recovery was in progress, but I wasn't there yet.

• • •

I met Todd at an informational meeting for my Tribe support group for veterans. He had recently returned to church after decades away, and he was clearly hesitant to join the group. The pastor and several others had encouraged him to visit, and he'd eventually decided to check it out.

In the Tribe group format, our fifth session is when everyone shares their story. By this point, Todd had come to a place where he believed that God could give him relief from the memories of his past trauma. This is what he shared:

> Back in 2004, while in the Navy, I was serving in Bahrain. I was stationed aboard a ship with one of my best friends when he went with a group to investigate a suspicious boat in the area. Right before my eyes, the boat exploded, killing my friend and several others. That moment haunted me, but I did my best to bury my feelings.
>
> In 2007, I was involved in an incident chasing pirates. Our boat flipped, I hit my head, and I sustained a traumatic brain injury. The repercussions included severe headaches, mood swings, and memory loss.
>
> I never really spoke about either of these incidents to anyone, especially not to my wife. I justified my silence because I did not want to seem weak or let people know how dangerous my job was. Besides, what was there to talk about? I was fine, right? It was nothing I couldn't handle. Nobody would understand anyway.

He didn't realize the extent to which these incidents affected him or those close to him. His headaches impacted everything: his job, home life, and personal psyche. He was up at all hours with racing thoughts, nightmares, crying— you name it. He was a mess, but he confided in no one. He felt all alone.

His marriage failing, the prospect of divorce brought him to a breaking point. He finally approached the Department of Veterans Affairs for help. The VA diagnosed him with PTSD and bipolar II disorder, gave him some meds, and told him to meditate and return in a month.

"How do I learn to meditate?" he asked.

"Take a class."

The classes were several days long and offered only during the workweek, which only works if you don't have a job. The meds barely helped, and every month the VA changed them or told me that they take a while to take effect, so I should give them another month. This whole time, I was slipping further and further down into what I call my rabbit hole of isolation and depression. There were times I hid in my closet with my pistol, praying and crying until I fell asleep, only to wake up and resume my never-ending cycle of PTSD episodes.

It wasn't until a friend of mine invited me to church that I was able to find a way out of that rabbit hole. Taking a step toward God set into motion the events that changed everything. I'd grown up in the church but later walked away because I always felt inferior around the people there, as if I could never measure up to them and was always being judged. There was a mentality at the churches I attended that I had to clean myself up before I could come to God. I had not yet experienced the truth that no one can clean themselves up for God and it is only His grace and forgiveness that purifies us.

The experience at my friend's church, however, was different. The message was "come as you are," the music was different, and best of all, the people were different. Refreshing. Not long after I started attending, the head pastor and his wife shared the story of their struggle with her bipolar depression and migraines. I was shocked. I was keeping it a secret from everyone, but I had the very same issues. I was amazed that I wasn't the only one with this type of suffering! Their story didn't have a rosy ending with a special prayer that cured everything, but it was a story of faith and turning to God to receive comfort when things are at their worst. It offered hope, and I tried to cling to it as best as I could. Although my faith was weak, I was trying. It was all I had at that point.

The next major turning point in my life came one Sunday morning at church. Our small-groups leader ran up to me, eager to share some news. She told me about a new group called Tribe for veterans and first responders. "Not interested," I said. Soon after, a pastor came up to me and said, "I want you to meet Ellie Stevens. She runs Advancing Warriors International and is looking for facilitators to help with a support group called Tribe for vets and first responders." He introduced me to her. I thought, *Well, now I'm stuck listening to what she has to say.*

It wasn't your typical sales pitch. It was intriguing. What could she possibly know about PTSD and headaches and bipolar and all the stuff I was dealing with? As it turns out . . . quite a lot. You know when God puts someone in your path as an answer to your prayers, only you don't know it yet? At the time, I told Ellie, "Sounds good. I will think about it." Translation: *There is no way on earth I am doing any of that.* I walked away figuring I was done with that and with her. *Whew, that was close!* Even the conversation had been way out of my comfort zone.

I don't remember exactly how the rest happened—I blame my TBI—but there were texts and what I'll call "in-person harassment" from the pastor and small-groups leader. The group was so stuck in my head that I decided to go and see what it was all about, mostly to satisfy my curiosity.

Seven people showed up at that first Tribe session. Todd had no idea what to expect, but he did have a lot of skepticism. As he suspected, it was way, *way* out of his comfort zone, but he stuck with it. We started the meeting with prayer, introductions, and a brief overview. Everything from that point forward reinforced leaning on Jesus for strength, not striving in your own power, and most of all, finding peace in the Lord.

Peace seemed to be the major lesson for me. Peace hadn't existed in my life for as far back as I could remember. I realized that this was exactly what I was missing: a clear program backed up by something powerful—by God. He spoke to all of us in Tribe, through Bible passages, Ellie, and each other. I quickly built trust in these people and in Jesus. We were all in the same boat, some worse off than others, but all hurting just the same. To my surprise, I shared things I had never discussed with anyone else, including the incidents that had haunted me for a long time. Just being able to talk about them was freeing.

When I look back at where I was then—lost, broken, scared, suicidal, with nowhere to turn—to where I am now, it seems long ago and far away. God has performed wonders in my life. His grace has given me hope and peace. Things aren't perfect; I still live with the effects of the TBI and still have trials. However, I now know that God's grace is sufficient and there is always somewhere or someone to turn to. Lean on Him, and He will provide comfort.

The fellowship among our group and with Ellie continues to this day and has taught me a lot about myself and about God. I have a better understanding of and closeness to Him. My pursuit of healing and peace became my pursuit of God. My personal growth continues as well. I'm thankful for the Tribe program, the people in it, and my mentor in Christ, Ellie.

Todd's pathway to healing began with his acceptance of an invitation to church, one small step toward God. His goal of finding relief from his pain, mental anguish, and grief turned into a pursuit of the "God of all comfort" (2 Corinthians 1:3). He was able to find the right medication regimen for his depression and work through the negative beliefs he was holding on to that were destructive to his faith.

He didn't have to prove his worth, because Christ's sacrifice had already done that for him. He didn't have to transform himself, but rather allow God to do the transforming. He had once thought that people suffered because they were being punished, but eventually he realized that suffering occurs even when people don't bring it upon themselves. He had lived most of his life believing that he deserved everything bad that had happened to him. No wonder he didn't want to go to church and be judged.

• • •

Todd's lightbulb moment happened when he was participating in a Tribe group meeting and the discussion turned to matters of the heart. We were talking about the differences between a heart set on proving one's worth through service and clean living versus a heart that depends on the Lord to make us clean. "We come as we are," I said. "God does the transforming work—not us."

As I diagrammed the differences on a whiteboard, Todd looked at me with his head tilted. "Why hasn't anyone explained it like this before?" he asked. This concept was a game changer. We were deconstructing one of the barriers that had once kept him away from church. He felt neither worthy of God's love nor good enough to be a follower of Christ. In that moment, however, he realized that God's assessment is the only one that matters. He was now free to live a life in pursuit of God—to seek after the One who had long pursued him.

Todd found a pathway to healing from his trauma by . . .

Making a move in the direction of God. Todd's first step was a very simple one: He accepted an invitation to church. Although he was a skeptic at heart, he decided to see what God had to offer. It took a while, but he wasn't disappointed.

Stepping out of his comfort zone. Had Todd not agreed to try something new, he would still be stuck in that rabbit hole. But he wanted so badly to escape his misery that he was willing to be uncomfortable if it would lead to recovery. I believe that if we are always comfortable, we are probably not where we need to be as Christians. We sometimes need to leave our comfort zones and depend on God's work in our lives. The more Todd stepped out of his comfort zone, the more God increased his faith and hope for the future.

Giving up the chase. Todd was so focused on finding relief for his pain that each time he hit a dead end it was devastating. In a way, God was his last and only remaining hope. The more he learned about the heart of God, the more he fell in love with God Himself. As he pursued the Healer and Giver of peace instead of healing and peace themselves, his healing and peace soon followed.

Drawing closer to God. As Todd's faith increased, the enemy's ability to sow seeds of shame, guilt, doubt, and loneliness diminished. He learned more about God's Word, which enabled him to recognize and dismiss the enemy's lies. He learned more about God's character and his own identity. He let go of old thought patterns and learned to stop relying on his own strength.

• • •

The Lord is closer than we can imagine, and He is waiting to receive anyone who pursues Him. The pursuit of God involves . . .

Recognizing the sacrifice that demonstrated God's love for us. Romans 8:32 tells us, "He who did not spare his own Son but gave him up for us all, how will he not also with him graciously give us all things?" Jesus conquered sin, death, shame, Satan, and hell itself through His suffering on the cross and His resurrection from the dead. This realization needs to redefine and reshape everything in our lives. The fleeting pursuits of this world lose their luster in light of the fact that we have everlasting life and access to the Creator.

Receiving and giving forgiveness. Once we understand that God will stop at nothing to demonstrate His love for us, it's time for us to receive His forgiveness. People tend to pull away from God when trying to cover up their sins, redeem their failings, or atone for their mistakes. That's what Adam and Eve did after they sinned in the Garden. However, when we see that God awaits us with open arms full of forgiveness (as illustrated in the story of the Prodigal Son), we are encouraged to welcome His embrace.

Renewing one's mind with Scripture. Hebrews 4:12 tells us, "The word of God is living and active, sharper than any two-edged sword, piercing to the division of soul and of spirit, of joints and of marrow, and discerning the thoughts and intentions of the heart." God's Word gives us the ability to take down arguments, lies, and deceptions from the enemy. According to 2 Corinthians 10:4-5, "the weapons of our warfare are not of the flesh but have divine power to destroy strongholds. We destroy arguments and every lofty opinion raised against the knowledge of God, and take every thought captive to obey Christ." No matter what you've believed in the past about your value and worth, allow Scripture to renew your mind and convey the truth about your identity.

Building trust in God first and then in others through community. This is a gradual process as we move away from the isolation caused by trauma or relational betrayals. We tend to hide from potential threats, like uncertain relationships and the fear of failure, in order to protect ourselves. God, however, calls us to step out in faith. He prepares the way for us, but it is up to us to follow His path. Psalm 37:23 tells us, "The steps of a man are established by the LORD, when he delights in his way." Ephesians 2:10 says, "We are his workmanship, created in Christ Jesus for good works, which God prepared beforehand, that we should walk in them." This means we can have confidence that God will go with us and prepare the way as we follow Him. As we trust Him with small things, we learn soon enough that we can trust Him with much greater things. Exercising our faith is like building muscle, but the ultimate power comes from the object, not the amount. And the more we trust God, the more our protective shells begin will to dissipate and the better we will be at interacting with His people as part of a community.

Surrendering achievements as a means of proving one's worth. This means resting in God's sacrifice. James wrote about how strong our desires can be and how quickly they can overcome our pursuit of God: "Desire when it has conceived gives birth to sin, and sin when it is fully grown brings forth death" (James 1:15). In this passage, the Greek word *epithymia* signifies an exaggerated or very strong desire. If our desires are prioritized above God, they will eventually end in death. We must learn to recognize anything that may be an *epithymia* and surrender it to the Lord.

God can take our mess and turn it into a beautiful story of restoration. No sin is too great for Him to redeem. No valley is so dark or so deep that He can't find us in it and bring us back to the light. We are children of an incredible God who loves us with an everlasting love. Please join me in prayer:

Lord, I pray that You will fuel me with Your love and quench my thirst with Your goodness. I will never stop singing Your praises. Overwhelm me with Your presence, and fill my mouth with Your words. Let my voice speak of Your greatness, and let my being testify to Your love, light, peace, joy, and power in everything that I do. I will never stop following after You!

REFLECTION

1. Which areas of your life do you devote the majority of your time, attention, and talents to? (These are likely the areas at greatest risk of becoming idols in your life.)
2. What are you afraid of giving up or losing, and why?
3. In what areas of life are you living independent of God's influence?
4. How have you experienced God's faithfulness?

CHALLENGE

Commit to setting aside time each day to meet with God intentionally, expectantly, vulnerably, and free from distractions. Spend time in the Bible and in prayer. Receive humbly His guidance, forgiveness, and peace. This time is your opportunity to be open and honest, baring your soul to the One who cares about you.

pathways to healing:
implementing self-care

When I was training to be a physician, I typically worked seventeen-hour shifts, lost a lot of sleep, and barely had breaks to eat. The entire culture of medical school was to focus on the patient first and yourself last. Much the same mentality exists in other fields of service where duty comes first, such as emergency services and the military.

But we hear the opposite message when we engage in air travel: Put on your own oxygen mask first so that you will be better able to help someone else. It makes sense when we think about it, but how often do we neglect taking care of ourselves with the notion that we are doing a service to others? If we neglect self-care as a pathway to healing, not only will we diminish our own performance, but others around us will likely also suffer as a result.

Self-care isn't glamorous, but it is an absolutely necessary part of healing from trauma. Self-care can include (but is not limited to) eating a healthy diet, prioritizing exercise and sleep, having good hygiene, reducing noise, effectively processing emotions, making allowances for downtime, and maintaining the level of self-awareness necessary to recognize barriers that might arise. The trouble is that many of us cheat ourselves in the area of self-care. Taking time to rest and recharge can make us feel like we're wasting time and sacrificing productivity.

For some people, it's a question of control. We want to be in control at all times, though that's simply not possible. Trying to control matters that are beyond our control is a much bigger waste of time and productivity than prioritizing self-care. This reminds me of American theologian Reinhold Niebuhr's well-known Serenity Prayer: "God, grant me the serenity to accept the things I cannot change, the courage to change the things I can, and the wisdom to know the difference."

Plenty of people engage in more obvious types of physical self-care these days as more research emerges about the importance of nutrition and exercise, but many neglect the emotional and spiritual aspects, including rest. Despite the well-publicized benefits of sleep many people still view getting enough rest as only a luxury, or at least not a priority. The spiritual and emotional aspects of self-care might also involve setting aside time and a safe space to process anger, hurt, or grief after a loss or even a difficult shift at work. Processing emotions is not a matter of stuffing them down but rather of asking God for help by doing things like praying and journaling.

A higher level of self-care could mean finding a support group or therapist with whom to process emotions, especially if they're related to past trauma. Making a point of addressing these issues has the added benefit of improving other relationships, since the fallout of unprocessed emotions often lands on those closest to us. In other words: If we care about our loved ones, we'll care for ourselves.

* * *

Chris is a firefighter who showed up at a church-based Tribe group for veterans and first responders. He seemed very reserved for the first few weeks, which is not at all unusual for someone in his field. You won't last long as a first responder if you can't remain controlled, calm, and collected during even the most strenuous circumstances.

Firefighters and paramedics are often first on the scene at some of the most traumatic kinds of emergencies. Especially in big cities, regular encounters with suicide, heart attacks, and gruesome auto accidents are part of a typical day at the office. First responders go home to family members who don't understand or can't relate and then return the next day to experience it all over again. This ongoing cycle leads to a compounding trauma effect, leading many to turn to substance abuse or other vices to help deaden the reality of what they face at work.

Most of us view firefighters as heroes who regularly put their lives on the line for others. But do we really understand what they deal with each day? It's difficult to imagine the trauma of pulling someone from a burning building, especially an infant or young child, or rescuing an elderly driver from a mangled car wreck. Not everyone survives, and that includes fellow firefighters. A simple mistake can have deadly consequences.

Performance is paramount among first responders. Any vulnerability is seen as weakness, and weakness can jeopardize a career, so firefighters and paramedics search for coping mechanisms that will get them through the day. Lighthearted humor turns dark. The occasional drink becomes a daily habit. Coworkers who once spoke freely no longer trust each other with their personal issues. No one wants to acknowledge the impact of their trauma.

There's no time to process trauma in the field, so the only option is to suppress and ignore any and all emotions until the job is done. Once emotions are stuffed down, however, they are often locked away for good, sometimes never to be addressed again.

Chris had not yet addressed his trauma when he began attending the Tribe meetings. I watched his demeanor slowly shift with each session—from reserved to contemplative to engaged. Things really changed for him during week four, when the group considered questions about control.

His lightbulb moment happened when, for the first time in his life, he realized that he placed the outcome of every emergency call on his own shoulders, internalizing the guilt and blame for not keeping people alive. Reflecting on this epiphany, he said, "Do you know what the survival rate is for a cardiac arrest outside of a hospital? Less than 10 percent."

Despite these statistics, he had been blaming himself whenever a patient didn't survive. As he looked around the room at the other group members, he said, "Wow, this really changes things!"

He was finally able to see the unreasonable pressure he'd been placing on himself throughout his career, and this recognition allowed him to release the burden he was carrying. From that point on, he knew that the only things he could control were showing up, doing what he was trained to do, and leaving others' lives in God's hands. As we progressed through the remaining Tribe sessions, he shared more openly and appeared lighter, freer, and more confident.

Chris found a pathway to healing from his trauma by . . .

Joining a group. Chris made the effort to find and join a support group in order to connect with others and with God. As a result, he found a group that shared both his faith and many of the same issues he was facing. Many people feel that groups are just not for them, but God has created us for community. Chris took a leap of faith, joined a group of people he barely knew, and was greatly rewarded for it.

Doing the work. Chris really invested in the program, engaged with Scripture, and attentively listened to other participants in the group. In so doing, he maximized the benefits of his Tribe experience. He applied what he learned about control to his life and realized how his misconceptions had kept him from finding peace and satisfaction in his profession.

Opening up. Had Chris not wrestled openly with blaming himself for every life lost while on the job, he wouldn't have recognized the flaws in his reasoning. As he increasingly shared his thoughts with the group, he was able to better understand which circumstances were truly outside of his control.

• • •

A significant aspect of self-care is learning to identify your triggers—and then developing a strategy to deal with them. Once again, a *trigger* is something that sets off a fight-or-flight reaction, brings on PTSD symptoms, or produces excessive stress. Especially when trauma is involved, it's vital to recognize your own triggers as well as the triggers of those around you. That doesn't mean you'll be able to avoid those triggers completely, but it better prepares you to handle them in the best possible way.

For example, some people with PTSD have a strong reaction when they feel trapped. It is important for them to know that there is a clear exit. I have treated people whose spouses have blocked the door to prevent them from leaving during an argument. Even when the spouse means well, the truth is that few people can trigger you like your significant other—the person you are probably around the most and likely knows you best. When things get heated, it's better to allow both parties to exit the situation and come together later when they can both think clearly and won't be reactive or defensive.

It's also a good idea to prepare in advance for situations

when you anticipate encountering a trigger. This involves knowing your physical and emotional limitations, as well as how your body reacts in certain environments. For example, if you've been involved in a serious auto accident and sometimes become tense when you're in a car (I know the feeling!), it is important to use relaxation methods while driving, like breathing exercises, singing, and prayer. If you become angry when you're hungry, it's important to carry snacks with you. In my case, I occasionally still deal with chronic pain, migraines, and irritability, particularly when I don't get quality rest. Therefore, optimizing sleep patterns is crucial for me.

Self-care is actually just a component in maintaining overall health. Self-care tools and strategies can promote relaxation and mindfulness in the heat of a stressful moment. Such tools might include journaling, listening to calming music, or reciting memorized Scripture. Such strategies might involve prioritizing time to rest, reducing the noise around you, and—like Jesus did—finding time to get away from others to connect with the Father.

It often feels like the day is over before we know it, especially with all the distractions we face and tasks we need to accomplish. However, when we set aside time to be alone with God and His Word, it's often the most important part of our day. It's an opportunity to process our feelings with Him without worrying about everything else in our lives. Whether we're sharing our anger, frustration, sadness, or grief, being alone with God is a safe space we all need.

• • •

I met Josh through a Tribe group for first responders. A law enforcement officer, he was seeking relief from trauma and anger he had carried for years. He kept quiet during the first few sessions—quiet but tense. As far as I could tell, he was taking it all in.

I had no idea.

Week one, I introduced a "barriers chart" to the group. I encouraged all of them to identify at least one barrier to work through and told them we would create an action plan during week four. When we got to week four, Josh mentioned that he had already stopped chewing tobacco—a longtime addiction of his—and had started praying and studying the Bible regularly with his fellow officers. As we progressed through the full eight weeks, I could see a significant change in his demeanor. He appeared looser and more laid-back. He laughed more and smiled more. Even his facial expressions were more relaxed!

As his comfort level increased, he shared more of his story. He grew up in an abusive household; his father was a raging alcoholic who became violent and destructive whenever he drank. Even as Josh fought the urge to end his father's abuse with one final, violent act, he continued to protect his mother from his father's rage. And whenever he stepped in his father's path, he paid for it with a beating. He did everything he could to protect his siblings and everyone he could from his father, but his mother refused to leave, despite his pleas.

His troubled upbringing had a large influence on his decision to join the police department. He was fiercely determined to protect the innocent and lock up those who preyed on them. He vowed to oppose the evil and darkness of the world, but he soon realized that he had his own darkness and evil to deal with. Like many other officers, the more corruption he encountered, the more he turned to defense mechanisms like alcohol and other distractions—anything he could find to avoid the pain of his past and the wickedness he saw on the job.

But nothing could take it away. He used his anger as a means of coping with his own vulnerabilities, or whenever he felt powerless in a given situation. No matter what he tried, however, he remained miserable. He was fighting a losing battle.

As I've said before, many first responders are hesitant to share their struggles for fear that they would be admitting weakness. But Josh pushed through that hesitancy and found the courage to join a support group of like-minded individuals. He put his desire for healing before his reputation, and he was rewarded for it.

When the program concluded, he said that the Tribe group had helped him release the traumas of his past and reconcile relationships that he'd felt had been completely destroyed. "My heart feels full and resurrected," he said. In fact, he enjoyed the Tribe group experience so much that he decided to become a facilitator.

He was also able to forgive his father, reconcile with his mother, and cultivate a healthier relationship with his girlfriend.

The "heart of stone" he had developed during his childhood was replaced with a "heart of flesh" (see Ezekiel 36:26).

Josh found a pathway to healing from his trauma by . . .

Acknowledging his need for help. Many law enforcement officers think they have to bury their traumatic struggles because they don't want anyone to know their emotional issues or see them as anything less than a powerful presence in their field, but Josh overcame this and found freedom.

Joining a support group. There remains a concern among first responders that confronting the trauma they've been exposed to could lead to the unraveling of their personal lives. But one benefit of support groups like Tribe is that, in addition to being confidential, they are based on the healing power, grace, and forgiveness of God. And God-centered groups promote freedom and transformation instead of weakness and disorder.

Trusting God and others. As Josh began to view Tribe as an authentic community of safety and compassion, he knew he could open up and trust his fellow group members, many of whom were dealing with similar issues.

Taking action. It's one thing to acknowledge the influence of past trauma; it's another to actually deal with it. Josh not only formulated a plan and committed to it, but he also stuck with it for as long as it took. He committed to walking with God daily in his work, in his relationships, and when no one was watching. He invested in self-care and emotional healing. And that's when everything began to fall into place.

• • •

What made the biggest difference in my own self-care journey was finding a therapist who understood and shared my faith. She helped me uncover the hidden motives of my heart and break the power of my self-denial. But the truth was that I'd still been holding back. If I really wanted to deal with my emotions, if I truly wanted to heal—and, just as important, if I wanted to help others heal—then I needed to deal with the trauma of my past sexual assaults.

I went back to my therapist and finally told her about the rape. As I shared what had happened, it was like I could feel the darkness all around me. I felt filthy. Dirty. I began to weep. I was no longer Ellie Stevens, but Eve in the Garden. Naked and ashamed.

Once I was done, after I'd told my therapist everything, we bowed our heads and prayed. In that moment, I felt God's presence comfort me. I sensed Him whispering truths to my soul: My identity was not in what had happened to me. My identity was in Christ, and I had been redeemed. I was His, and He was mine. His peace was not just a blanket, but a covering for my nakedness.

We spent subsequent sessions dealing not only with the rape but also with the trauma I had buried much deeper and for much longer: the molestation I had suffered as a child. My moral wound had begun with the molestation and continued to build with every instance of sexual trauma that had followed. Each time, I'd lost more and more of my perceived innocence.

As we continued to process my past, I recalled shifting from being a confident, carefree child who felt loved and accepted to feeling lost and lacking confidence, as if I would never be enough. I remembered unexplained tears and not wanting to attend school. I feared the loss of my family and felt distant from everyone around me. I didn't know how to delight in God because I couldn't imagine His delight in me.

It took my Christian therapist to convince me that I was pleasing to God. She asked me to imagine myself as radiant and spotless. I closed my eyes and pictured myself once again as that carefree child, before I was tainted by the evil of others. I imagined myself running into the arms of my loving heavenly Father. He embraced me, and I knew at that moment how much I was desired, accepted, and fully loved.

My righteousness, I recognized, comes from God alone. This realization helped free me from the grip of the enemy, from his constant accusations that I was filthy and undesirable. I had long known in my head that Christ's sacrifice made me spotless and innocent before God, but now I believed it in my heart. I could sense it. I could feel it. It was tangible, accessible, and oh, so amazing!

My awe of God—my childlike wonder—was reawakened for the first time in many, many years. At the same time, my irritability, self-hatred, impatience, and rigidity began to diminish. I again discovered what it was like to delight in God as I experienced Him delighting in me. What's more, He reconfigured my thinking: My quest to find fulfillment in a man faded away as my soul found satisfaction in my Lord.

• • •

I'm the first to admit that self-care, taking time to rest, and listening to my body have never been my strong suit. But I had no choice if I wanted to recover. I had to implement new strategies when I crashed and burned, when I couldn't handle the slightest stress. As someone used to staying productive and constantly engaged in physical activity, nearly three years of not working left me barely able to look at a computer or even sit and listen to people talk. I had to schedule extra time to rest and learn relaxation techniques. I also had to learn what my triggers were, since I'd never paid attention to them before.

One of my triggers is traffic. I've been rear-ended while stopped at stoplights on four different occasions. When I go for a drive, my body automatically tenses up. I've discovered that I need a strategy just to get in a car. I listen to encouraging Christian music, focus on positive things, and incorporate breathing techniques while driving.

Another trigger I've discovered through therapy is related to my sense of smell. I was sitting in our living room one day when my roommate started cooking bacon and sausage. For reasons I didn't understand, I was extremely restless. I felt trapped in my own home and like I needed to escape. Then my restlessness turned to rage. I ended up leaving the house for a while in order to cool down. I had no idea what had come over me.

The next day, I told my therapist about this intense, out-of-the-blue anger. As we discussed the experience, it reminded me of a similar scenario when I'd been staying at my ex-boyfriend's apartment. His roommate, I recalled, had cooked sausage and bacon almost every morning. I had no grasp of the power of olfactory memories before that moment. Smells, I learned, are closely tied to memories.

Some people have fond memories attached to smells, such as cookies baking in the oven, hot chicken soup on a cold day, or a freshly cut lawn. When odors are associated with traumas or bad memories, however, it can turn a good day into a terror. Once I recognized this trigger, I processed it with my therapist. Breakfast meats no longer have any power over me! This was how I realized the importance of implementing a strategy for dealing with triggers.

One of the best self-care strategies is to develop your own wellness team. This involves identifying a few dependable, trustworthy people with whom you are willing to be vulnerable. These are people you can call in the middle of the night for help but who will also tell it like it is with love and grace. Your wellness team should be composed of people who want the best for you—those who will sharpen, encourage, offer accountability, and provide support in the midst of trials and temptations. In other words, they should be the type of people who live out 1 Thessalonians 5:11: "Encourage one another and build one another up, just as you are doing."

Many people are focused on helping others but not themselves. But the principle communicated by flight attendants also pertains to self-care: The healthier we are ourselves, the better we can assist others.

It's one thing to talk and think about self-care; it's another to make a plan and commit to it. One of the best ways to do this involves accountability. In the Tribe program and Advancing Warriors International, we begin by identifying a goal, and then we implement a strategy to overcome a specific barrier to healing. Each participant identifies a barrier to healing in a spiritual, physical, relational, or emotional area and a plan of attack to address it.

Empowered by God and encouraged by their fellow Tribe members, many group participants have enjoyed tremendous success. I've been surprised by how quickly change can happen when people are both motivated and supported. Josh was a great example of this. By the end of the program, his action plan to quit chewing tobacco had been successful, and he hasn't done it since.

It's important to find an activity, place, or experience that helps reduce or even eliminate distractions. Some people like fly fishing; others like a cozy seat by a fire. For me, it is hiking in the mountains. With no phone signal, I no longer have the distractions of social media, emails, or texts. Completely unplugged is the best way for me to clear my head and escape the noise. I can see how King David was able to write several of his psalms early on while he was out in the fields tending sheep.

Hiking is my preferred way of connecting with God on a deep level, focusing on the beauty of His creation, and meditating on His Word. With no distractions, I can be present, mindful, and engaged in connecting with Him intimately. I typically find a large rock or a space off the beaten path to pray and listen. One day, in Colorado's Snowmass Wilderness area, I found a large rock and sat on it, gazing up at Snowmass Mountain. I met with God surrounded by the beauty of the fall colors. The contrast of the snow on the mountain peak was breathtaking.

As I prayed, I asked God what He wanted me to know. That's when I got a powerful sense that I no longer needed to protect myself. He would be my protector. Tears streamed down my face because I knew that's what I'd been trying to do. I'd been on guard against letting people into my life thanks to my history of betrayal. Because of all the distrust I'd built up, I was obsessed with trying to maintain control.

I learned an incredible lesson in the mountains that day, one I never would have learned had I not set aside time and space for just me and God. I learned that He is my protector, that—no matter what happens—I do not have to be afraid. I might face more trauma someday, but I trust Him with my future. I want to spend my time helping others find Him and His love. The freedom that came with my lesson that day was indescribable, and the moment made a lasting impression on my soul.

● ● ●

Working with my therapist, I uncovered the pain from my sexual assault and the stress my body was carrying—stress that had contributed to my inflammation, chronic pain, and migraines. I explored areas of my life where I was very hard on myself, and I continued learning how to rest in God. In dealing with my trauma, I was able to let go of anger, resentment, and bitterness and receive God's love and grace.

This process was difficult yet necessary, and it had a very positive effect on my physical symptoms. For months, expectations had been my worst enemies. I felt like my body was betraying me by not cooperating. *Why don't I respond to treatment?* In essence, I was fighting against myself. Confronting my trauma helped me realize just how interconnected the mind, body, and soul all are, and I learned to accept my physical limitations and stop pushing myself so hard.

As I reflect on what I wrote on that significant plane ride back to Colorado, I realize that God had truly answered my prayers. He had helped me view my situation through spiritual eyes and see that nothing we go through in life is wasted. When it felt like God had put me on a shelf and I was no longer usable, He'd actually been training and preparing me to help hurting people in ways I never could have imagined.

I had been emphasizing my physical recovery, but God was more concerned with healing my soul and refining my character. He revealed deeper wounds that I needed to prioritize ahead of my physical issues. As the emotional and spiritual healing slowly came, the physical healing followed. I learned that with God we can do all things, and without Him we can do nothing (see Philippians 4:11-13 and John 15:5). His healing is far superior to any healing I had in mind.

REFLECTION

1. What is one self-care tool or theme you can implement an action plan around? Use the acronym *SMART* to help develop your strategy: Make your plan *specific, measurable, achievable, relevant,* and *timely.*

2. What is an area of your life that you are trying to gain control over? Is this area something that you can actually control? If not, how can you surrender your misguided effort and give it over to the One who ultimately does have control?

3. What is one of your major triggers? How and when did it begin affecting you? Explore the origins of that trigger with God, loved ones, and/or a therapist. How might you diminish its power in your life?

CHALLENGE

Commit to a self-care plan that treats your body as God's temple. Reduce excessive noise and address any barriers that hinder your relationships, your walk with God, and the plan He has for you.

pathways to healing:
a supportive community

The word *hypocrite* comes from the Greek word *hypokrites*, meaning "an interpreter from underneath." Ancient Greek actors often wore masks to interpret different characters or take on a counterfeit persona.

I sometimes wonder what we've learned over the past couple of millennia, since this is how many of us still live today. We try to pretend we have it all together. We post only the best, most flattering updates on social media, leaving out the messiness of daily life.

I especially see this behavior among the community of first responders, where there is a heightened desire to keep private lives private. First responders often don't like others knowing about their business. They encounter trauma on a regular basis but don't want to admit to being affected by the violent and disturbing calls. No one wants to be seen as weak. The result is a culture permeated by judgment, ridicule, and distrust. These dedicated workers convey the notion that they simply "move past" the trauma and don't let it bother them.

As if that were even possible.

Too many first responders won't even share their feelings with loved ones—either because they don't want to bring their trauma home or because they're convinced that no one else can understand what they go through. Of course, this only perpetuates their feelings of isolation, fueling the potential for addiction and further detachment. What many of these folks need is a supportive community that gives them the opportunity to discuss these issues freely.

I've heard first responders and veterans say that they avoid support groups because they think talking about their problems will just make things worse. They also don't want to participate in one-upping sessions where a bunch of alpha types compete to share the most traumatic experience. Some groups just end up discussing sports, hunting, or politics, persistently avoiding the real issues.

I agree that simply talking about their problems won't get them very far. When support group meetings become venting sessions where people only feed off each other's misery, not much healing takes place. If group members are constantly sizing each other up as if they are in a competition, that won't work either. However, if they are able to process their experiences together and work through the barriers they face, that can be a game changer—even more so if they are able to implement a faith-based approach. The body of Christ is meant to be an encouraging community of believers. As the biblical book of Hebrews says, "let us consider how to stir up one another to love and good works, not neglecting to meet together, as is the habit of some, but encouraging one another, and all the more as you see the Day drawing near" (Hebrews 10:24-25).

In addition to this admonition that churches not neglect gatherings, Hebrews also tells us to encourage one another daily in the truth: "Exhort one another every day, as long as it is called 'today,' that none of you may be hardened by the deceitfulness of sin" (Hebrews 3:13). But how can this happen effectively in a culture where people spend more time texting than meeting together, in a society where few seem to want to be known? In a world of people constantly hiding their vulnerabilities and flaws, how does anyone know what to say to demonstrate encouragement or exhortation?

• • •

Jen had recently moved to Colorado when a fellow veteran encouraged me to connect with her. I learned that she was struggling with isolation and searching for a solid spiritual community in the Denver area. When I first met her, she shared her desire to get connected and further explore her faith. She had participated in various support groups through the VA, but they had seemed superficial to her and like they were characterized by an underlying sense of competition. Moreover, they didn't address matters of faith or Scripture. She was looking for something different.

Like me, she had spent much of her life seeking self-assurance. While she had confidence in her character and abilities, she craved belonging, appreciation, and acceptance. She had tried to soak up every experience that might help her enjoy life and enjoy other people but had invariably ended up in traumatic and/or toxic environments. Instead of attaining self-assurance, she'd remained stuck—in her mind, a failure. She'd fallen into the trap of trying to be someone others had expected or wanted her to be, and now she spent her time trying to mend what had been broken.

When you experience trauma, your mind often creates a false truth, one that doesn't align with reality. You develop negative beliefs about yourself and the world around you. You lose your sense of safety. You lose yourself. You might exhibit behaviors that are out of character with your personal values and beliefs. These behaviors only serve to cement the negative beliefs, pulling you further away from your true self. The original pursuit of acceptance leaves you feeling alienated and powerless.

So how do you rebuild when life depletes your self-assurance? How do you find your way back? *Is* there even a way back? And if there isn't a way back, is there a way forward—a way to rebuild a new and stronger version of you, one that better aligns with your true self?

I believe so. I believe it begins with recognizing that God is the source of our assurance.

Jen's decision to seek this pathway changed everything. Not only did she seek God on her own, but she also found others with whom to pursue Him together. She joined a Tribe meeting for veterans at a local church and embraced the opportunity to open up her heart and her past to the group. Together, they asked God to help them heal. This is her powerful story of transformation:

> I grew up in a broken family, dirt poor and suffering many traumatic events before the age of eighteen. I tried to escape my hometown by accepting a job that included a lot of travel, but at the age of nineteen, I was abducted from a hotel and held for a couple of days while two men raped me. This experience shook me, but it also drove me to the decision that I wanted more out of life.
>
> In 2005, I joined the Marines. I wanted to challenge myself, find my true strength, and be surrounded by people who held honor, courage, and commitment as their core values. I had faced a lot up to that point, but I still wasn't broken. I still believed in myself and in people. However, I wasn't what some might describe as a "real" Marine. I was often told, "You're too nice to be a Marine." I wasn't aggressive enough. I wasn't the fastest or the strongest. I was young, guarded, and foolish. But I was also determined, resilient, and hardworking.
>
> After all is said and done, I'm proud of my service. I loved wearing my uniform. I love my country. But that doesn't mean it wasn't hard.

During her four years of service, Jen endured frequent sexual harassment, which made her believe that she didn't belong. She shipped out to Iraq, where she remained for the majority of her deployment. She spent a month volunteering with a team of women who searched Iraqi females and children for weapons. It was during that assignment that she lost a fellow Marine to a suicide bomber:

[The loss] hit our platoon hard, and I struggled with survivor's guilt. Shortly after returning from deployment, I was raped by a fellow service member, something I didn't tell anyone about until I spoke with a therapist after I got out. I was heartbroken that I had to face this kind of trauma again, because I had joined the Marines to be surrounded by better people than those I'd encountered before. (That's not to say that I didn't serve with some amazing Marines. There were more good than bad, and I'm still friends with many of them.)

My deployment and survivor's guilt were difficult, but the sexual trauma cut the deepest. I lost myself, my self-worth, and my direction. I lost faith in people and in God. In the aftermath, I acted out by drinking and making poor choices with men. I ended up having an abortion. I wouldn't let anyone get close. I wouldn't let anyone get to know the real me. I put on a happy mask, hoping no one could see what was hidden underneath. I was drowning in shame, guilt, and grief, just trying to survive and find a sense of normal.

Her sense of worth in free fall, she entered a relationship with a fellow Marine who made her feel lovable. They broke up multiple times over a year of dating, mostly because she didn't feel good about the relationship. But she ignored the red flags and married him, both because she was afraid to be alone and because she didn't think anyone else would love her:

I was broken. But I felt lucky. At least *he* loved me. These were the self-beliefs that led me to say yes to a marriage that I knew deep down wasn't right for me.

Then I started to feel trapped in that marriage. My husband became controlling, telling me who I could hang out with and where I could go. He told me I had to get out of the Marines or he would divorce me. (More red flags!)

I completed my enlistment with an honorable discharge but lost even more of my sense of purpose and independence. I tried to focus on being the perfect wife, cooking and cleaning, playing the part. I made brownies for him at midnight and smoked marijuana because he asked me to, even though I hated it. I just wanted to make him happy. I felt more and more unlike myself, more trapped.

Then I started acting out in my marriage. I made secret purchases and went out drinking when my husband was away at training—anything to make me feel like I had some sort of control over my own life. Unfortunately, one of those nights when he was gone, I was the victim of a home invasion, robbery, and rape. When he returned from training the next morning, I was at the hospital getting a rape kit. He wouldn't even meet me there. He couldn't believe I had allowed this to happen. His exact words were "This doesn't happen to normal people," and I believed him.

I contemplated suicide the following day. He found me in the bathtub with a razor to my wrist and stopped me. For that I'm grateful. He picked me up and held me as I cried. That was the last time he held me.

Our marriage did not survive. He asked for a divorce three months later, and I moved out a week after that. He found someone new soon after. I felt like a discarded piece of trash, traded in for something shiny, new, and unbroken. This was my tipping point. I was shattered. There were many, many more events that depleted my sense of self, but this specific one was the straw that broke the camel's back. I fell apart, hard.

About two weeks later, she was alone in bed. The furnishings in her bare apartment consisted of the bed, a cardboard box, and a television set. Her life had hit rock bottom. She began to cry, she says—not just a quiet sob, but "that soul-shaking cry that makes your body feel like it could burst into a million pieces, only to scatter across the universe, lost forever."

I know that sounds dramatic, but that's how I felt. Just as I was about to fall apart completely, the room suddenly went still. The air, the energy, everything . . . just still. I felt what was like the warmth of a hand on my left cheek. Immediately, my entire body went calm. I felt complete and utter peace for a brief moment in time. I knew God was letting me know that He was there and I was not alone. He had me.

Yes, I'd had faith before then, but God had always felt distant. My faith before had been this thing that I should believe in, mostly so that things would go right and I would go to heaven. But that night, I felt God. I know He's real. I know He loves me. I know that no matter what, He has me. I can endure anything because I will never be alone. I will always have this deep well of strength and peace to draw from.

I am currently eleven years down the road from my divorce and those traumatic events. Looking back, it's like I was dropped unceremoniously into the fire—a fire that helps create weapons, like the furnace a swordsmith uses. I lost all shape and purpose. The subsequent years were when God began His hammering and chiseling. I still don't know what the final product looks like, but I believe that I am hardening with a strength only He can give, like steel that can endure any battle. This is a forging of character, not a hardening of the heart. He is forming me into a weapon of faith for His purposes.

I haven't given Him an easy time of it. I've fought Him and rebelled. But the good news is that He is able to use the trauma, challenges, and pain of this fallen world to create good. He is shaping and strengthening me through it all. He is using the fire to forge me into my best self. I am grateful that He continues to work on me, that He hasn't given up on me. He creates beautiful things from tragic circumstances. He heals the hearts of the broken.

Jen's journey isn't over. She, like all of us, continues to struggle with sin and unwise choices. She is human. She hasn't been in a relationship since her divorce, mainly because she is still learning to trust again.

After moving to Colorado, I began hanging out with a toxic group of people. I fell into depression and gave in to my inner demons. The Tribe support group and Advancing Warriors saved me. They helped pull me out of the darkness and introduced me to an amazing community of people who understood my pain and trauma. They shared my faith. They shared my fears and doubts. They accepted and loved me. They trusted me with their stories and listened to mine without judgment. I learned who I am as a child of God. I no longer feel pressure to prove that I'm worthy of His love.

If you are reading this, I'm guessing that you, too, have experienced trauma in your life. I am so sorry you have endured hard things. And yet, as much as I empathize with you and wish that none of us had to experience these heartaches or endure such tragedies, I believe that those who experience the most pain often experience the most growth. God can work wonders in your heart. He can heal your brokenness and your wounds. He can craft you into a warrior. "And we know that for those who love God all things work together for good, for those who are called according to his purpose" (Romans 8:28).

Yes, it will take strength and perseverance, patience and faith. I believe in God's ability to transform you, and I believe you are capable of being transformed! Especially if you are a veteran or first responder, please seek out a support group. Allow yourself to be vulnerable. Allow yourself to belong. Find a supportive, faith-based group of people who will fight right alongside you in your spiritual battles.

● ● ●

Weeping uncontrollably in her barren apartment, Jen was at her lowest point and felt utterly alone. That's when she had a transcendent experience with God, sensing His presence in her life in a way she never had before. This moment demonstrated to her that she was never alone—that, even at her worst moment, she was worthy of receiving comfort from her Savior.

Jen found a pathway to healing from her trauma by . . .

Recognizing that her goals were mistaken. Jen was chasing self-assurance, mistakenly viewing her "true self" through the eyes of the world. She had to reach a point where she stopped looking to others for validation and acceptance.

Refocusing her pursuit. Instead of constantly trying to fit in with the wrong crowd, Jen shifted her priorities to finding like-minded people who could encourage her in both faith and recovery.

Joining an authentic community. Jen sought out a Tribe group of veterans in order to find connection and support. What she found was a group centered around Jesus Christ and focused on allowing God to accomplish the work of transformation in their lives.

Removing the mask. Once she was part of a supportive, empathetic community, Jen felt empowered to remove her happy mask and truly be herself. She shared with the group about the broken parts of her life and invited God to fill her with His love and comfort.

Engaging with her community. It's one thing to check out a support group, to dip a toe in the water. It's another thing altogether to truly engage with it—to open up and allow yourself to be known. Jen dove right in, actively working through her own issues while inspiring others along the way. Her community gave her the strength and encouragement she needed to overcome the trauma she'd faced.

•   •   •

I began my private practice with the mentality that God would bring along just the right patients—people He would heal and transform through me. From the start, I was prayerful about each patient, and I've been able to pray with many of them. My stamina was low to begin with, so I started out slow and gradually increased my workload.

Throughout my first year, I witnessed some amazing results. My first patient saw his symptoms subside within four months. (This was particularly crucial, since he had told me, "If I am not better by December, I will end my life.") God helped me navigate many stressful situations. People who had nearly given up saw their faith and hope restored. God showed up in incredible ways, and I was awestruck.

But there were plenty of occasions when my patients didn't tolerate treatment well or were still hitting barriers. I knew it took time and patience to treat serious mental illness, to overcome years of maladaptive behaviors or break down subconscious walls, but I internalized every perceived failure and took all of them personally. It took more visits with my therapist to see what I was doing to myself and to eventually surrender the results to God.

During this chapter in my life, I learned that my role is to show up, to hold things loosely, and to partner with

God. If I compare my work to a waltz, then I need to let Him lead. He goes before me. He follows behind me. He is "a shield about me" (Psalm 3:3). He prepares me for what lies ahead.

• • •

I've learned how important it is for followers of Jesus to sharpen, strengthen, and encourage one another to keep the faith, but the truth is that for a long time I lacked genuine community in my life, starting when I left home for college. That's not because it wasn't possible; rather, it's because I was unwilling to become vulnerable and transparent with myself, let alone with others. The one person who truly knew me was my mother, and she was the only family member I allowed inside.

For most of my life, my only experiences with groups had been class projects and sports teams. And in those cases, there had always been a specific and limited objective and no need to go deeper than that. I came across a nonprofit called My Quiet Cave when I first moved to Colorado in 2014, and that was my first glimpse into being part of an authentic community. My Quiet Cave helps support emotional health from a Christian perspective, providing a safe community to pursue both mental and spiritual wellness. It leads people who struggle with mental-health issues—or have loved ones who do—through a nine-week program focusing on hope, connection, education, and identity in Christ.

I began working with My Quiet Cave groups almost right away, and—because in their model leaders share first—I began to open up about my story. At first, however, I kept things on a surface level. I never delved too deeply. But that all changed the more I got involved. I watched as people who entered a group feeling isolated and disconnected went on to achieve amazing personal growth. I witnessed healing take place that would have been nearly impossible with individual therapy or medication alone. As I continued working with My Quiet Cave and later joined the organization's board, I recognized the need for veterans and first responders to have this same kind of community.

I didn't realize it at the time, but I wasn't yet ready to cultivate this type of community for myself. I wasn't living an authentic life. I was still wearing too many masks.

Working through my multiple traumas, the pain and suffering slowly burned through my protective layers. I could no longer hide behind my past achievements, skills, or strength. I was powerless. Exposed. And that was ultimately a good thing: What was finally exposed could finally be dealt with. Only I couldn't deal with it alone. I learned to let God take the lead, and He sent some amazing individuals across my path. Through my journey, the power of God's Word and the lessons I learned from my own trauma led me to create Tribe, my group curriculum for veterans and first responders.

Tribe incorporates lots of Scripture to help trauma sufferers explore the Bible in ways that make sense to them. They are able to examine their pasts within a community of like-minded participants and facilitators. They learn about the power of God's love and begin breaking down walls of resistance and barriers to recovery. It is important for participants to know that the program is Christ-centered; we focus on following Jesus and seeking wisdom from the Holy Spirit. Participants who see transformation in others begin trusting the Lord again and then also trusting others. There are no hidden agendas or judgments. There is no competition. Instead, there is a culture of building up and encouraging other Tribe members to pursue (or keep pursuing) God. They work together to expose issues they have stuffed down, sometimes for decades.

Even as first responders and the military implement more programs designed to preserve mental health, the general mindset in these fields is still *No one needs to know about my stuff*. The fear persists that if others know about one's so-called dirty laundry—if it's aired in front of everyone—then it might jeopardize their career. Unfortunately, instead of a fellowship, these fields remain more like groups of silos.

• • •

Jack is a seasoned paramedic and firefighter who contacted me looking for psychiatric help. He began developing PTSD symptoms after responding to a couple of particularly upsetting calls, and he didn't know what to do. In the first case, a teenage girl was involved in a collision with another first responder and was killed on impact. Since the girl was the same age as Jack's son, this call hit closer to home than usual.

Later that same month, he responded to another dead-on-arrival call, this one involving an infant. At this point, he started experiencing intense anxiety and even flashbacks of the infant's face. He found me via a Google search and noticed that I, too, was a veteran. He wanted someone to talk to, but he didn't want anyone from his fire station to know what he was dealing with—the nightmares, panic attacks, and hypervigilance. If he admitted these things to his coworkers, he feared, he would be seen as weak.

He was resistant to join a faith-based group because his faith was minimal, if that. He was also reluctant at first to discuss the issues he was facing with his peers, but by this point, he was willing to try anything. Deep down, he understood that the only way to find healing was by exploring the trauma of his past.

He'd grown up without a father, and his mother hadn't shown much affection. She'd been dealing with her own unresolved traumas, and at times Jack had felt like he was essentially raising himself. His teenage years were perilous, and he was headed down a dark path that would likely lead to prison.

That all changed when he discovered paramedicine. He enjoyed the fast pace of the work, and he liked helping people in urgent need. He didn't realize it at the time, but even then he was subconsciously trying to control his surroundings. Meanwhile, his PTSD symptoms went unnoticed for decades.

His situation came to a head after he got divorced and his ex-wife and son relocated to another state. Jack wanted a new start, so he, too, decided to make a move. He remarried and ended up as a paramedic in the same state as his son. Things were going along reasonably well until those two difficult calls . . . and that's when his misguided pattern of false control and ignoring past trauma finally caught up with him.

He went looking online for help and came across the website for my practice. He noticed that I work with first responders, and I told him about an upcoming Tribe group for professionals like him. Once he got past his initial reluctance, he decided to join the support group and begin individual treatment. The deciding factor was a conversation his wife had with a stranger.

His wife had just returned from a trip where the man sitting next to her on the airplane was a firefighter. He told her that he had struggled for years with some of the things he'd witnessed on the job and that it had really helped to talk with other first responders about it. She told Jack about her airplane encounter, and she encouraged him to join the trauma support group. Thanks to this encouragement, he started to wonder if the group might prove beneficial after all. He wondered if God was trying to tell him something.

As his therapy progressed, he reported feeling more at peace. He recognized that he wasn't responsible for controlling everything going on around him, nor could he be. Instead, he began trusting God, and the pressure he had imposed on himself for a lifetime started to fade away. The more Scripture he read, the more it made sense to him. As his faith in Christ deepened, his PTSD symptoms weakened.

Empowered by his positive experience with Tribe, he felt like it was time to tell his coworkers at the fire station what he was doing. He no longer felt the need to hide his emotions, and this attitude gave him the confidence to be himself around his fellow firefighters. He said that the sense of vulnerability and camaraderie he enjoyed at the Tribe meetings had encouraged him to let down his guard and become truly known by others, many of whom were dealing with similar trauma.

Jack found a pathway to healing from his trauma by . . .

Seeking out his peers. Despite his negative perceptions, Jack knew there was a potential benefit to gathering with fellow first responders. Sometimes it requires a leap of faith (or a feeling of *I'll try anything*) for a reluctant individual to give a support group a chance. And when Jack found a group that followed Jesus and His example, it made all the difference.

Removing his mask. Jack decided to take off the disguises he'd worn for years while simply trying to survive and hold everything together. When he finally began to reveal his failures, mistakes, and pain from the past, he experienced peace.

Letting go of control. Jack's PTSD symptoms showed him that he didn't have the control he wanted—not even close. After he accepted that reality, he was able to begin trusting God with his future, for forgiveness, and to be his protector.

Serving as an example. Once he'd become part of a supportive community, Jack was able to share his experiences with the other people at his fire station. They were able to see for themselves his newfound openness and authenticity. He also brought this perspective home with him, which helped the rest of his family become more honest, transparent, and authentic.

● ● ●

One of Tribe's goals is to help people connect with God and other Christ followers so that they might then spread this authentic way of living to their families, coworkers, and communities. In the beginning, a new Tribe group often consists of individuals who treasure their privacy and wear a multitude of masks as a means of self-protection, but the curriculum is designed to show the participants that their efforts at protection are actually working against their healing and recovery, keeping them from a life of freedom and personal growth.

It's my hope that at the end of eight Tribe sessions the participants will share what they've learned with others in their lives. As I've said before, trauma doesn't just affect veterans and first responders. Finding a supportive community is good for everyone, and we can all benefit from dealing with the painful hurts of the past.

One final note: If you can't find an organized support group in your area, consider the idea that authentic community can also be found within a family unit. For example, when spouses are truly committed to one another, to unconditional love and ongoing forgiveness, their marriage can serve as a beautiful picture of the gospel in ordinary life. The process of healing from trauma will benefit a person's entire family because he or she will no longer be constantly on the defensive nor triggered by seemingly innocent interactions. When your loved ones treat you with understanding and compassion, you will be more likely to let go of resentment and unforgiveness. In other words, you will be more likely to heal.

REFLECTION

1. Are you currently part of an authentic community? If so, how can you expand it? If not, what can you do to address this need?
2. What are the accomplishments, labels, positions, or identities you hide behind in order to keep your vulnerabilities hidden?

CHALLENGE

Identify at least one person in your life to meet with once a week—someone who can sharpen you, hold you accountable, and know the *real* you. But don't just think about setting up a regular meeting. Commit to a time and place. Make it happen.

CHAPTER THIRTEEN

pathways to healing: holding on to hope

In this hope we were saved. Now hope that is seen is not hope. For who hopes for what he sees? But if we hope for what we do not see, we wait for it with patience.

ROMANS 8:24-25

Hope is many things: the expectation that a longing will come to fruition; the desire that a loved one will recover from an illness; the yearning that someday your dreams will come true. Hope can grow and waver over time depending on one's life circumstances and emotional state, but we never want to lose all sense of hope.

Holding on to hope is a significant pathway to healing. Holding on to hope means making a commitment to focus on the positive outcomes in the midst of the trials. Research has shown that hope is essentially the opposite of anxiety. People who hold on to hope tend to view both their external and internal environments in ways that prevent chronic anxiety problems. In the world of trauma healing, research shows that a hopeful mindset is a significant factor in helping childhood trauma survivors recover and flourish.[1]

When people lose hope, there is little motivation to seek help or pursue healing. Whether it's the hope that they will eventually get better or the hope that the traumas they've faced will equip them to help others, holding on to hope is an integral component on the path to recovery. The Bible tells us in Hebrews 11:1 that faith is the assurance that things hoped for will come to pass. The apostle Paul specifically writes about having hope in eternal life and patiently awaiting the day we will see our Savior face to face: "Now we see in a mirror dimly, but then face to face. Now I know in part; then I shall know fully, even as I have been fully known" (1 Corinthians 13:12). We also hope in God's promises for this life, such as the promise that "for those who love God all things work together for good, for those who are called according to his purpose" (Romans 8:28) and Jesus' promise of the Holy Spirit: "I will ask the Father, and he will give you another Helper, to be with you forever" (John 14:16). Finally, Paul reassures us, "I can do all things through him who strengthens me" (Philippians 4:13).

The sense of hope found in these promises offers peace and joy that no amount of suffering can extinguish. This hope is what my uncle held on to through a brutal war. His hope was fueled by his faith; no matter whether he lived or died, he knew God was with him and working for his good.

• • •

My uncle Tom played an integral role in my decision to join the Air Force, fueling my passion for serving military members and veterans. He grew up attending church and learning about Jesus, and he can still recall watching the regular baptisms.

"I asked my mother what that was about," he said, "and she told me it was for people who believe in Jesus. And I said, 'I want to do it!' That was so unlike me—to do anything that brought attention to myself."

He was about eight years old at the time, and he continued to be a happy child for several years. But then his father died when he was a teenager, and from that point forward, he no longer had a male role model. He rarely talked about how his dad's unexpected death affected him. He neither wanted nor expected sympathy, so he simply put the experience behind him.

"I could never fully come to terms with why God let him die," he said. "I became rebellious and lived a worldly life, but my heart was grieving because I felt separated from God."

He barely graduated high school due to the loss of direction in his life. He decided to leave home, to escape, so he joined the United States Army at the earliest possible opportunity. The Vietnam War was going on at the time, and his placement scores earned him an invitation to helicopter pilot school. He initially declined because he had no knowledge of helicopters nor any desire to fly them, but he changed his mind when he learned that the invitation meant that he could depart for training the very next day. Before he knew it, he was a lead helicopter pilot at age twenty.

It was apparent that he would need to adapt quickly to this high-pressure role if he wanted to stay alive—and keep as many other soldiers alive as possible. He lost many of his fellow pilots to combat missions, including his best friend and former stateside roommate. He was routinely forced to make life-and-death decisions for himself and his flight crew, for the formation of other choppers following him, and for the soldiers under enemy fire on the ground who needed support or medical evacuation. On the occasions when he was unable to answer a call for help, he rarely knew if assistance ever came.

There are no templates or guidebooks for the horrors of war. Tom racked up more than 2,100 hours of combat flight time and received sixty-six medals for his service, but he still felt like he was in over his head. He watched as a fellow soldier was shot for trying to flee from his duty. He had no choice but to follow orders and take each day one at a time.

Despite the chaos, destruction, and death all around him, he never forgot his childhood faith and the demonstrations of God's power he'd witnessed. Those moments helped affirm his beliefs and gave him the hope he needed to stay alive and mentally intact. He said that one of those events occurred on the darkest night of his life:

Looking back over my two tours in Vietnam, I suppose I had more than a few close calls with tragedy. In every situation I had to deal with, I relied heavily on my faith in God to pull me through. Such was the case late in my first tour flying helicopters in Vietnam. My role was to lead a flight of ten UH-1 [Huey helicopters] conducting combat assaults.

For one particular mission, his helicopter was restricted from night flying due to some inoperable flight instruments. Daytime flying was no problem, but flying in darkness or heavy cloud cover was extremely difficult, if not impossible, without these instruments. It was also monsoon season in Vietnam, with rain expected every afternoon while heat-intensified storms severely restricted the helicopters' ability to fly safely.

Whenever the storms affected our flight path, we typically diverted or landed and waited until the danger passed. On this day, we had delays due to storms, and it became apparent to me that our mission would likely require us to continue to fly past sunset. We encountered a widespread storm, and I was forced to select a tree-lined clearing large enough to accommodate our flight of ten choppers.

The delay on the ground took us well into hours of darkness. I was in a precarious position—I could not safely fly until the skies had cleared and there was sufficient moonlight to give me a reference to the ground and the horizon. Adding to our problems was the fact that we had landed in an area of known enemy activity. Almost immediately after we got the call to take off, we observed tracer rounds coming at us through the darkness.

His flight group lifted off together in a tight formation, with each aircraft following closely behind the helicopter in front. Tom used his searchlight until he had safely climbed above tree level.

About the time I saw the trees pass directly under me, my helicopter entered the clouds, and I had no reference point to tell me how to fly. The aircraft to my rear immediately radioed in a panicked voice, telling me, "You're in a steep left bank!" I'd had no idea. I couldn't recall a darker or blacker night, and at that moment, I called out to God for help. I knew that unless there was a miracle, my helicopter would inevitably crash, along with the helicopters following me.

My desperate cry was answered immediately. A thin line appeared on the horizon in front of me. Evidently, I had climbed into an area between two layers of dense clouds. The light was from Biên Hòa (our destination) and was filtering between the cloud layers from approximately sixty miles away.

The strip of light was very thin, and the only way to see it was if my helicopter remained at a steady altitude. I discovered that I lost sight of this reference if I climbed or descended by more than fifty feet. With the light providing the required horizon and illuminating my path, I led our formation home safely.

I firmly believe that God was watching over me and protecting me during my many hours of combat flight time. I asked Him daily to do just that, and I had faith that He would. He never failed me.

Tom followed the light on the horizon all the way home. He led ten helicopters out of the darkness and out of the war zone. His faith that God would get him through the worst of times was reaffirmed. The event strengthened his dependence on God in all that he did—not only in war, but also later on in life. This moment was priceless to him, one he will never forget.

It wasn't the quality or quantity of his faith that saved him that night but the object of his faith. He'd grown up going to church, but in the combat zone he experienced Jesus' love, grace, and power in tangible ways. The faith he began with continued to be built, and his hope in God as his protector remained throughout his life. His hope in God also spared him from developing hypervigilance, nightmares, and major relational stressors.

Tom is one of the rare exceptions—a veteran of the Vietnam War who has been married for forty-five years without succumbing to addiction or severe PTSD. He enjoyed a great military career after Vietnam, though he did endure more trauma and loss in Iraq during the Operation Desert Storm era. He went on to become a senior executive with the Federal Aviation Administration, and he now volunteers with a prison ministry, is a wonderful example to his twelve grandchildren, and serves as a facilitator for the Tribe program.

● ● ●

Tom's pathway to wholeness involved holding on to hope. Even when he lost direction in life, he never gave up on his faith. Hebrews 11:1 says that faith is "the assurance of things hoped for, the conviction of things not seen." The writer then describes Scripture's leading men and women of faith as a "great . . . cloud of witnesses" (Hebrews 12:1). The chapter that follows, sometimes called the Hall of Faith, tells the stories of Old Testament saints who lived not by their own strength but by their hope that God would demonstrate His power through them.

I view my uncle as an example of a great witness in my life, not looking down from heaven, but encouraging me in person toward the calling God has for me. He relied on his faith to overcome paralyzing fear, the chaos of combat, and the loss of multiple flight crews during his military career. Thanks to his faith, he was able to not simply survive the darkest of nights in the jungles of Vietnam but also to be refined by God into a great leader and man of character who today helps point others to the hope that he discovered.

Tom found healing by . . .

Exercising his faith. Tom trusted God first with his eternal salvation and then with his daily life. Many people believe in God to get them to heaven but lack the faith to turn to Him with every aspect of their lives. Though the circumstances were far from ideal, the war actually helped Tom jump-start his faith, and that faith only grew from there.

Giving up control. Tom's faith was not in some unknown higher power. He didn't rely on his own strength for success or even survival but on God's mercy. Many veterans leave combat zones with survivor's guilt—or just plain guilt—blaming themselves for what they could have done differently. Sure, Tom did what he could to survive, but he left the rest up to God. I believe that his reliance on God helped him avoid many of the mental wounds that combat often creates.

●　●　●

I have emphasized the vital role of faith in dealing with trauma, but believers are still susceptible to the symptoms of PTSD. No one knows the exact formula behind PTSD, and trusting God doesn't magically make trauma go away, but a strong and vital faith can help reduce the chances of developing severe PTSD or suicidal thoughts. Hope in God's unfailing love can get us through almost anything, and it will equip us to point others to Him.

When I was at my lowest—stuck in a broken relationship, unable to even read, facing the loss of my Air Force career—I had several choices before me. I could have become bitter or resentful, or I could have fallen into addiction as a form of avoidance and self-comfort. But I chose a third path: I held on to hope—hope that no matter what I went through, God would be able to redeem and restore my life. Unfortunately, I did become bitter and resentful at times, but I still clung to my Savior, even when my grip was failing. I thought about the apostle Paul's second letter to the Corinthians, where he writes, "This light momentary affliction is preparing for us an eternal weight of glory beyond all comparison" (2 Corinthians 4:17).

Paul endured beatings, stonings, shipwrecks, and betrayals throughout his life, but he looked back on his troubles as "light momentary affliction[s]." His faith gave me hope that God could somehow use my trials to produce a "weight of glory" within me, that He could still transform me to become more like Christ.

Romans 5:2-5 gave me extra fuel: "Through him we have also obtained access by faith into this grace in which we stand, and we rejoice in hope of the glory of God. Not only that, but we rejoice in our sufferings, knowing that suffering produces endurance, and endurance produces character, and character produces hope, and hope does not put us to shame, because God's love has been poured into our hearts through the Holy Spirit who has been given to us." And James 1:2-4 reassured me even further: "Count it all joy, my brothers, when you meet trials of various kinds, for you know that the testing of your faith produces steadfastness. And let steadfastness have its full effect, that you may be perfect and complete, lacking in nothing."

Few of us are able to actually rejoice in the midst of trauma and suffering. I certainly wasn't. Many times, it's all we can do to keep going. However, we can rejoice in the refining and shaping that is taking place. Most of all, we can rejoice in the fact that we will one day come face to face with our Savior and spend eternity with the lover of our souls.

Throughout my yearslong journey with trauma, I prayed that the experience wouldn't be wasted. I didn't want to emerge from my trials as the same person I'd been before. I wanted to be sharpened—finely honed. Holding on to hope despite my many setbacks ignited a refining fire that burned off my shame, self-righteousness, and pride. I had no choice but to mature in my faith. It was the worst time of my life, but it also initiated the greatest spiritual growth. This is what suffering can do if you choose the third path.

• • •

It's now been several years since I suffered my traumatic brain injury on the slopes of Longs Peak. In that time, I've seen God work in my life in powerful ways. He has strengthened my faith and increased my hope. I now gauge my well-being by how connected I am to Him. Am I focused on His goodness or on the negative aspects of my current situation? Am I restless, or am I at peace? And whenever I try to make things happen via my own strength, I am quickly reminded of my foolishness.

It's easy to get caught up in the stressors of this world, whether politics or a pandemic. However, if I remain anchored to God and His Word, holding tightly to His promises, nothing of this world can ruin me. Thanks to His goodness, I now have a space in the mountains where I lead training retreats for veterans and first responders. I see His healing power at work in the lives of the people He leads to me, and I witness His transforming power in their lives through Tribe group meetings. In recent years, He's allowed me to partner with several amazing leaders and work with them to share His love with a broken world.

I rejoice in helping others recover from their trauma, most of all because I've been there myself. I know what it feels like to suffocate in darkness, desperately clinging to a faint sliver of hope. I held on to that hope through the worst storms of my life, and I know that you can too. No matter how hard things get, don't give in to the darkness. No matter how hopeless it seems, God will make a way out. He will light your way through the storms if only you will let Him.

REFLECTION

1. When and where in your life have you experienced unprecedented growth? What spurred on that growth?
2. In 2 Corinthians 4:17, Paul describes his afflictions as "light" and "momentary." How can God help transform our perspective about the trials of life?
3. What is holding you back from the kind of faith that hopes for things yet unseen?

CHALLENGE

Prayerfully consider your life, taking time to examine various traumas or major events you've experienced. Invite the Holy Spirit to illuminate any underlying bitterness, resentment, anger, or unforgiveness from those traumas. Commit to letting go of bitterness, resentment, and anger from the past, and receive the freedom God offers. (This may need to be done with a therapist or other professional, depending on the extent of the trauma.)

purpose redeemed

As I'm writing these words, the news is filled with cover age of yet another mass shooting. Ten people—ten inno- cent people—were killed by a lone gunman at a Boulder, Colorado, grocery store. What makes this one particularly difficult for me is that I've shopped at that very store several times over the last few years.

This shooting is just one more example of the evil in our world that is hell-bent on destruction. Colorado has endured at least seven mass shootings since 1993, three of them among the most well-known cases in American history: the Columbine High School shooting, the Aurora theater shooting, and now the King Soopers grocery store shooting in Boulder.

Although I wasn't born in Colorado, it has been my home for seven years now. For a time, the Boulder gunman and I lived in the same city. The grocery store itself is just one block over from a friend's home, near a trail that I've frequently hiked. Just thinking about that makes me anxious. Honestly, I don't want to visit a grocery store anytime soon, and certainly not that one.

I've learned that my reaction to trauma triggers is often physiological. I mentioned this before, but thanks to my history of rear-end accidents, my body still tenses up whenever I get into a car, especially when I'm in heavy traffic or stopped at a red light. My neck muscles are chronically tense, as if I'm anticipating the next whiplash injury. I often experience similar sensations when wearing a mask in an enclosed building, because a situation where I'm unable to read facial expressions and nonverbal cues heightens my awareness and sense of insecurity.

I've also learned how to recognize when my body becomes reactive, when I need to work through my natural urge to avoid. The all-or-nothing behaviors of my past led to a life of fear, and the thoughts that came to my mind after this shooting threatened to revive those fears. Traumatic events, even when they don't involve us personally, can ignite a host of overwhelming emotions. They can immediately remind us of other tragic events, of lost lives and despair. Moreover, they make us face a choice: Give in to the fear and try to bury the pain or lean on God and process our emotions with a supportive community.

• • •

As I wrap up this book on trauma, the Boulder shooting reminds me that trauma is often just around the corner. It can occur at any time, in virtually any place. The threat exists at our churches, in our neighborhoods, right outside our front doors. No one is immune. Whether at a school, a theater, or a grocery store, the trauma of a public massacre hits close to home for many Americans. These places, after all, aren't supposed to be combat zones. They are supposed to be safe, for us and our loved ones.

After many months of isolation and social distancing due to a pandemic, many months spent living in fear of a virus, the local grocery store is one of the few places where people still must frequent. We all need food. We all have to eat. But for those who already experience public anxiety, simply going out in public with a bunch of mask-wearing strangers is already hard enough. An event like this at a place everyone needs to visit will surely foster an even greater resolve among trauma survivors to avoid and isolate. We wonder when another shooting will happen. Another car accident. Another attack. *Is any place safe?*

Trauma isn't limited to soldiers or first responders. The potential for it is all around us. Fires and floods. Rioting and violence. Tragic accidents. The deaths of loved ones. Future episodes of trauma could happen anywhere. But responding in a healthy way can build character and resilience as well as the empathy necessary to better help others. If we respond in an unhealthy way, however, we'll find ourselves in emotional turmoil. Then we won't be in a position to help anyone.

Followers of Christ are called not to shrink back in the face of tragedy but to provide God's comfort and peace to the hurting. When I learned the location of the Boulder shooting, I felt a surge of restlessness and anxiety along with an immediate desire to avoid public places. But I also felt a competing fire in my soul to help the individuals, families, and first responders who were impacted by the tragedy. I wanted to be a little bit of light in such a dark time. As the author of Hebrews tells us, "we are not of those who shrink back and are destroyed, but of those who have faith and preserve their souls" (Hebrews 10:39).

It is easy to focus on fear in a world shrouded in darkness, but we can still rise above the chaos to assist others. Few of us learned in school how to process negative emotions or deal with tragedy and loss, but those among us who have overcome our trauma have an opportunity to offer hope to those who haven't.

We are not called to avoidance but to boldness. Scripture encourages us to be both fierce comforters and fierce protectors of God's children. The Boulder police officer who lost his life in the shooting, Eric Talley, was reportedly a believer in Jesus Christ. Talley was following his Savior's example as he laid down his life to protect others.

Let us, too, follow Christ's example. When we are tempted to remain in our comfort zones, to stay in our protective bubbles, let us instead step out of our false sense of safety and help bring hope and healing to those who need it.

• • •

As I look back on my journey and the process of healing from my trauma, I see evidence of God's love and faithfulness all along the way, guiding me and keeping me on the right path. I still encounter barriers, and I certainly have plenty of room for additional growth and transformation, but the freedom, peace, and joy I now experience seemed unattainable just a few years ago. The pride I once felt—a sense of superiority regarding my education, for example—was exposed as self-righteousness. My traumatic experiences shattered the false identities I'd created, forcing me to confront my inadequacies and failure. And yet, even as I was laid low, God's love for me became more palpable than ever. My pride no longer prevents His love from reaching the deepest parts of my soul.

I'm convinced that God is using my own experience with trauma to make me a better psychiatrist. My years in medical school, my postgraduate training, my Air Force residency, and my subsequent fellowship—combined with the wisdom I received during the most difficult time in my life—have given me not only a deeper understanding of trauma and depression but also an extremely personal experience with the amazing comfort of God. Once I learned to let my walls down, I discovered what it felt like to have God wrap His loving arms around me. And receiving His comfort has equipped me to give comfort to others afflicted by trauma. I understand more than ever how trauma impacts relationships, thought patterns, emotions, and the soul, and I have a broader set of tools and techniques to help guide others toward healing.

I still suffer from migraines on occasion, and I continue to receive treatment and maintain appropriate self-care. I also still experience some PTSD symptoms, but the power they have over me is minimal due to the medical wisdom and spiritual understanding I've gained over the last several years. I'm now able to take a step back, evaluate emotional triggers, and ask God for help in reaching the next layer of healing.

Perhaps the biggest lesson I've learned through my trauma journey is that my deepest desires can only be met by God. With Him by my side, I can get through anything. His love for me is unwavering and never changes, even when I'm at my worst. I've also learned the value of using my sufferings to help others. My history of pain and heartache has actually been a benefit to my practice and my patients. (As we read in Psalm 126:5, "those who sow in tears shall reap with shouts of joy!") I can empathize with others, though I may not have experienced the same traumas or stressors they've faced. I'm able to offer genuine compassion as I walk alongside them.

Though I resented it at the time, the months of forced rest I experienced were in many ways for my good. I developed a deeper connection with the Lord when life's distractions were removed. Just as the prophet Elijah learned to hear God's still, small voice, I became able to connect more intimately with His Word. By the time my period of forced rest finally ended, I recognized the importance of setting aside time each day without distractions to read the Bible and pray.

God's Holy Spirit helped illuminate my self-deception, uncovering my unforgiveness and bitterness. I found a Christian therapist who helped me examine the hidden motives of my heart. (I had tried before with other mental-health professionals, but they hadn't shared my faith.) I learned to let go of the maladaptive behaviors she and I uncovered together. Finally, I was enabled to acknowledge the list of grievances I'd been keeping against others and myself. I needed to both forgive and receive forgiveness. Nowadays, I make a habit of asking God to reveal any unresolved trauma in my life.

With my therapist, I also discovered more about the power of community. Although it was a very compact community (just the two of us), the freedom I felt when I was honest with myself, her, and God was incredible. *This*, I thought, *is what the body of Christ is meant to be.* This small taste of community encouraged me to cultivate larger groups of people who could take off their masks and examine their self-deception together. This is how Tribe support groups were born.

• • •

My hope is that you have been encouraged by the stories and lessons in this book. Whether you have experienced personal trauma, deal with it in your line of work, or simply want to help others find healing, these action points are for you.

If you are a believer in Jesus Christ, you can have confidence that He is more than able to help you reach your full potential. Indeed, He is our example: He offered comfort and support everywhere He went. He is the most self-aware individual who has ever walked this earth. He took care of Himself, making time to rest and eat, pray and sleep. He surrounded Himself with a supportive community of disciples. And no one before or since has lived with a greater sense of purpose.

We, too, have much the same calling: To bring comfort to the brokenhearted (1 Thessalonians 5:11). To be self-aware (1 Peter 5:8). To practice self-care (1 Corinthians 3:16). To engage in community (Hebrews 10:24-25). To live with purpose (John 15:9). If we abide in Christ's love, then our mission and purpose will be fulfilled.

Remember these themes, and take action to pursue them:

Comfort and support. Many family members and friends of trauma sufferers are unable to adequately comfort their loved ones because they have not allowed themselves to receive comfort. The fear of confronting past wounds, failures, mistakes, or betrayals can perpetuate avoidance and create barriers that prevent us from receiving God's comfort. Moreover, every trauma is different. There is no hierarchy of traumatic experiences. Some dismiss their traumatic experiences as "not that bad," while others can't bear the thought of revisiting theirs. No matter what perspective we're coming from, the more our hearts are full of compassion, the more we will be able to provide comfort and support to those in need.

Self-awareness. A vital step on the path to recovery is acknowledging our traumas, stressors, and barriers. Only after these factors are exposed can they be dealt with effectively.

Many people who develop PTSD as adults have traumatic or stressful experiences in their pasts, often dating back to childhood. That's why it's important to not only process recent events but also revisit the past in order to address trauma that might have remained untouched for years.

Self-care. Regardless of how much or how little trauma someone has experienced, implementing self-care is critical to the healing process. Under the self-care umbrella reside things like developing better awareness and mindfulness skills; incorporating appropriate rest, nutrition, and exercise; and spending time with God. Self-care also includes creating and maintaining healthy relationships and necessary boundaries. Toxic relationships typically lead to negative behaviors, but once we understand how certain interactions have the power to trigger us, we are one step closer to facing our triggers and, eventually, overcoming them.

Community. People are not meant to live in isolation. We were created to act as a unified body. Christians are a community of believers, but we can only be a genuine community if we allow others to see the real us, not just what we want them to see. Just as we can't receive healing if we don't think we need healing, we can't be truly known unless we reveal our true selves. Being part of an authentic community gives us the freedom to encourage, strengthen, and sharpen one another. Our strengths can help others in their weaknesses, and we can learn to form relationships grounded in love, forgiveness, and reconciliation. Ecclesiastes 4:9-10 says, "Two are better than one, because they have a good reward for their toil. For if they fall, one will lift up his fellow. But woe to him who is alone when he falls and has not another to lift him up!"

Purpose. The prophet Isaiah, referring to the coming Messiah, said, "He was pierced for our transgressions; he was crushed for our iniquities; upon him was the chastisement that brought us peace, and with his wounds we are healed" (Isaiah 53:5). In other words, Jesus gave up everything in order to assume the burden and punishment for our sins so that through our faith in His sacrifice we can have eternal life with Him. He faced the punishment we deserved so that we might partake in God's gift of salvation. God's love knows no bounds. Let the Good News of the gospel dwell in your heart, and allow God to redeem your purpose.

•　•　•

God has endowed each one of us with distinct gifts and talents and has placed us into this world at this specific time. As you connect with God and lean on His faithfulness, let Him transform you into the person you were created to be. Though the enemy brings fiery trials, God can use that fire to refine you, shaping you into a vessel of love, compassion, and strength. And let us never forget that hurting people are all around us. Let's show them that God's healing grace is available to everyone.

I speak from experience: God can heal your trauma. He can redeem your pain and suffering. He can make you not just a survivor but an overcomer. He did it for me. He can do it for you.

notes

INTRODUCTION

1. American Psychiatric Association. *Diagnostic and Statistical Manual of Mental Disorders*, 5th ed. (Arlington, VA: American Psychiatric Association, 2013), 812.

CHAPTER 1

1. C. S. Lewis. *The Screwtape Letters* (New York: HarperCollins, 2001), 12.

CHAPTER 4

1. William Cowper. "Love Constraining to Obedience," in *The New Oxford Book of Christian Verse*, ed. Donald Davie (Oxford: Oxford University Press, 1981), 195–6.

CHAPTER 6

1. Robert Weiss. "The Prevalence of Porn." PsychCentral (May 22, 2013). https://www.psychcentral.com/blog/sex/2013/05/the-prevalence-of-porn.

CHAPTER 8

1. Pan American Health Organization (PAHO) and World Health Organization (WHO). https://www.who.int/news-room/fact-sheets/detail/suicide.

2. Centers for Disease Control and Prevention (CDC). https://www.cdc.gov /suicide/facts.

3. US Department of Veterans Affairs (VA). https://www.va.gov/opa/pressrel /pressrelease.cfm?id=5565.

CHAPTER 9

1. Bessel van der Kolk, MD. *The Body Keeps the Score* (New York: Penguin Books, 2015).

CHAPTER 13

1. R. T. Munoz, H. Hanks, and C. M. Hellman. "Hope and Resilience as Distinct Contributors to Psychological Flourishing among Childhood Trauma Survivors." *Traumatology* 26, no. 2 (2020): 177–84. https://doi .org/10.1037/trm0000224.